Heroic animals are
SMARTER than JACK

91 amazing true stories

D0951664

Helping animals & connecting animal lovers worldwide

The publisher
Smarter than Jack Limited (a subsidiary of Avocado Press Limited)
Australia: PO Box 170, Ferntree Gully, Victoria, 3156
Canada: PO Box 819, Tottenham, Ontario, L0G 1W0
New Zealand: PO Box 27003, Wellington
www.smarterthanjack.com

The creators
SMARTER than JACK series concept and creation: Jenny Campbell
Compilation and internal layout: Lisa Richardson
Cover design: DNA Design and Lisa Richardson
Cover photograph: © Rachael Hale Photography (New Zealand) Ltd 2005. All worldwide rights
reserved. Rachael Hale is a registered trademark of Rachael Hale Photography Limited.
www.rachaelhale.com
Illustrations: Amanda Dickson
Story selection: Jenny Campbell, Lisa Richardson, Anthea Kirk and Angela Robinson
Proofreading: Vicki Andrews (Animal Welfare in Print)
Administration: Anthea Kirk
Charity liason: Angela Robinson

The book trade distributors
Australia: Bookwise International
Canada: Publishers Group Canada
New Zealand: Addenda Publishing
United Kingdom: Airlift Book Company
United States of America: Publishers Group West

The legal details
First published 2006
ISBN 0-9582571-3-2
SMARTER than JACK is a trademark of Avocado Press Limited
Copyright © 2006 Avocado Press Limited

Contents

Responsible animal care

The stories in this book have been carefully reviewed to ensure that they do not promote the mistreatment of animals in any way.

It is important to note, however, that animal care practices can vary substantially from country to country, and often depend on factors such as climate, population density, predators, disease control, local by-laws and social norms. Animal care practices can also change considerably over time; in some instances, practices considered perfectly acceptable many years ago are now considered unacceptable.

Therefore, some of the stories in this book may involve animals in situations that are not normally condoned in your community. We strongly advise that you consult with your local animal welfare charity if you are in any way unsure about the best way to look after animals in your care.

You may also find, when reading these stories, that you can learn from other people's (often unfortunate) mistakes. We also advise that you take care to ensure your pet does not eat poisonous plants or other dangerous substances, and do not give any animal alcohol. In some rather extreme cases, you may even need to monitor what television channels your pet watches!

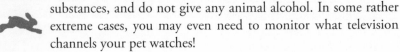

Creating your SMARTER than JACK

Heroic animals are SMARTER than JACK is a heart-warming book that celebrates the heroic animals in our lives. You will read true stories about animals using their intelligence to rescue and help others, prevent tragedies, and take care of people and other animals.

Many talented and generous people have had a hand in the creation of this book. This includes everyone who submitted a story, and especially those who had a story selected as this provided the content for this inspiring book. The people who gave us constructive feedback on earlier books and cover design, and those who participated in our research, helped us make this book even better.

The people at the participating animal welfare charities assisted us greatly and were wonderful to work with. Profit from sales will help these animal welfare charities in their admirable quest to improve animal welfare.

Bob Kerridge wrote the moving foreword, Lisa Richardson compiled the stories, did the internal layout and helped with the cover design, Rachael Hale Photography provided the beautiful cover photograph, Anthea Kirk and Angela Robinson helped with selecting the stories, Vicki Andrews did the proofreading and Amanda Dickson drew the lovely illustrations.

Thanks to bookstores for making this book widely available to our readers, and thanks to readers for purchasing this book and for enjoying it and for giving it to others as gifts.

Lastly, I cannot forget my endearing companion Ford the cat. Ford is now 12 years old and has been by my side all the way through the inspiring SMARTER than JACK journey.

We hope you enjoy **Heroic animals are SMARTER than JACK** – and we hope that many animals and people benefit from it.

Jenny Campbell
Creator of SMARTER than JACK

The enchanting cover photo

Masquerading behind the adoring expressions of our much loved pets are the stories and adventures, capers and escapades that have endeared them to our hearts and made them all a special part of the family.

This wonderful new edition of stories about everyday animals is brought to life with the enchanting cover photograph by renowned photographer Rachael Hale. Her distinctive images, famous around the world, capture the character and personality of her favourite friends, while allowing her to continue to support her favourite charity, the SPCA.

With the success of this series of animal anecdotes now established in New Zealand, Australia, the United Kingdom and North America, perhaps the best story is that the sale of every book makes a generous contribution to animal welfare in that country.

Rachael Hale Photography is proud to be associated with the SMARTER than JACK book series and trusts you'll enjoy these heart-warming stories that create such cherished images of our pets, along with the delightful pictures that tell such wonderful stories themselves.

www.rachaelhale.com

The delightful illustrations

The illustrations at the bottom of this book's pages are the work of Amanda Dickson. Amanda (27) is the human retainer and devotee of her Balinese cat Miss Tilburnia Cairo Casbah (9).

When not serving Miss Tilburnia, Amanda can be found reading, watching films and, most often, drawing. Amanda is a trained cartoon animator with four years' experience in the field who has now turned her hand to book illustration.

Amanda can be contacted by email at mandsmail@gmail.com.

Connecting animal lovers worldwide

Our readers and story contributors love to share their experiences and adventures with other like-minded people. So to help them along we've added a few new features to our books.

You can now write direct to many of the contributors about your experiences with the animals in your life. Some contributors have included their contact details with their story. If an email address is given and you don't have access to the internet, just write a letter and send it via us and we'll be happy to send it on.

Throughout the book we have included other ways you can be involved with SMARTER than JACK – tell us about an amazing animal charity in your community, a smart person you know, your questions about animals' behaviour, or your favourite story in this book, or send us a photo of your animal with a SMARTER than JACK book. We also welcome your letters for our 'Your say' section.

Do you like to write to friends and family by mail? In the back of this book we've included some special SMARTER than JACK story postcards. Why not keep in touch and spread the smart animal word at the same time.

Since 2002 the popular SMARTER than JACK series has helped raise over NZ$320,000 for animal welfare charities. It is now helping animals in Canada, the United States of America, Australia, New Zealand and the United Kingdom.

The future of the SMARTER than JACK series holds a number of exciting books – there will be ones about cheeky and sassy animals, rescued animals and baby animals. You can subscribe to the series now too.

If you've had an amazing encounter with a smart animal we'd love to read about it. Story submission information is on page 145. You may also like to sign up to receive the Story of the Week for a bit of inspiration – visit www.smarterthanjack.com.

Jenny's endearing companion Ford the cat

Foreword

One of the most stupid things a person can say is to refer to animals as being 'dumb', but how often we hear it!

Clearly these people have never lived with animals and experienced their wily ways and unique characteristics. Likewise they have obviously never thumbed through any of these delightful books where it is blatantly apparent that, rather than being 'dumb', animals are indeed 'smarter than Jack'!

Working with animals as I do, I have had many opportunities to observe just how smart they can be when they want to be. I have encountered unabashed examples of our resident cats and dogs selling themselves to the passing parade of strangers who come to our SPCA Animal Village with a view to adopting one of them.

The cats resort to a number of tactics, ranging from extending a paw through the bars of the cage to hook anyone who may be walking by, to rolling unashamedly on their backs purring loudly, to 'buffing' the cage door in reckless abandon to reveal how passionate they are, to sitting coyly and pathetically at the rear of the cage to appeal to a sympathetic passer-by.

And the dogs are no better. They use their round brown eyes to gaze lovingly into those human eyes that are gazing back, luring them under their spell (some even resort to shedding a tear at the appropriate time when someone is obviously spellbound). The puppies, of course, are notorious for seeking attention as they jostle with their litter brothers and sisters to be 'the one', while there is always one really smart one who stands aloof looking pathetic (they are always the first ones to be chosen).

Whatever the tactic used, the human target is selected and is 'fair game', usually succumbing to the pitiful plea to be taken home ... now, that's smart!

However, their genius doesn't stop there. It's what they do with you in your own home that really elevates their talents to new levels, and it is here that the real stories evolve. I wonder how many spouses have declared 'that animal will not take over this house', only to become pure marshmallow, succumbing to an animal's every demand; or how many beds have been commandeered by the hairy ones to the extent that the human occupants have to resort to new sleeping positions so as not to disturb the lead weight that refuses to be moved … that's smart! These pages abound with smart stories that are told best by the writers with personal stories to recount.

And, dear reader, as you may have experienced for yourself, the real proof of animals' genius is in their ability to steal a chunk of your heart while they are with you, and take that little bit of you with them when they finally pass on and 'cross the Rainbow Bridge'. Anyone that can do that has to be really smart (and beautiful).

Bob Kerridge
Chief Executive
SPCA Auckland
New Zealand

Bob and his special friend Merlin

1

Heroic animals are devoted

A real asset to our family

For 15 years we had a wonderful golden-eyed tabby cat named Bruno. He was such an asset to our family and very tolerant of children and other pets.

I didn't realise what an important part of the family he was until I was recuperating from foot surgery. On most nights, my husband and son would retire for the evening before I would. Bruno would usually stay by my side and keep me company. Then when I turned off the TV and lights he would disappear. Once I got to the stairs he'd be there waiting for me.

I had not learned how to safely navigate stairs with crutches. Instead, I'd go along backwards on my backside, dragging the crutches along. Bruno would always be one or two stairs above me, watching me and encouraging me upwards.

It was only when I was safely up the long steep flight that he would leave me and attend to his own business. This continued every night of the many weeks I had crutches. I don't know who was more relieved when I finally graduated to a walking cast – me or Bruno!

Donna Kuffler
Calgary, Alberta
Canada

Bruno looked after Donna

Benji earned his biggest gold star

Karen, my friend of many years, used to live on her family's horse farm. She has since married and left, but continues to visit her parents and ride their Morgan horses.

This is a story told to me by Karen and her family.

One day about 15 years ago, Karen was walking to the back field to check on the horses, when she noticed they were along the fence line where the neighbours' stallion was also standing. Not being afraid of practically anything, Karen walked up to the fence to be with the horses. She was talking to them all as she often does, and on this day included the stallion in her conversation.

At some point something must have spooked the neighbours' horse, and he kicked his back legs up. Karen had been close to the fence at that moment and had turned around just in time to catch the horse's hoof right in her eye. With the kick being so strong it knocked her to the ground, and we think she was unconscious for quite some time. Her eye was swollen shut and bleeding.

Now comes the heroic part of the story.

Benji, the family's golden retriever (who in his own right could fill a book on all the things that can go wrong for a dog on a farm, as there were many accidents that involved him – but that's another story), had wandered into the back field at some point, and found Karen lying on the ground.

Karen says she remembers him licking her face until she had enough sense to realise it was him. He guided himself around her several times to encourage her to grab his tail, and once she had a hold of him he slowly and carefully, with all the patience in the world, led her back to the house. For those who know what the back fields of a farm are like, you know it can be very rocky and bumpy, with small hills and 'pot holes'. We think it must have taken them several hours to get back.

3

Benji, their loving family dog, had saved her and what good sense he had shown in leading her back home! It just goes to show how intelligent dogs can be. He knew she needed help and led her to the source of that help.

Karen, as I remember, had to wear a patch over her eye for some time and also had many stitches. To this day she still has a scar from the event.

Benji has since passed away, but we reminisce often about all the amazing and funny incidents that involved him, with this event being the one to earn him the biggest gold star you can imagine.

Jennifer Thomasen
Kingston, Ontario
Canada

Tiger was a true gentleman

I have many true animal tales to tell, having had animals for many years. Some have gone to pet heaven and some are still here on Earth.

A particular pet who comes to mind is Tiger, a handsome tabby cat with a big build, long whiskers and a charming gentlemanly way about him.

In the mornings Tiger would come in and sit on my bed, get my attention and then hold out his paw for me to shake. He would do this until I got up and gave him his breakfast. He also used to follow me everywhere I went.

At the time of this story I was a young mother, waiting for a taxi on a chilly day with my daughter, then two years old. Tiger crossed the road to where I was waiting and 'talked' to me until the taxi came. He saw me into the taxi and smartly walked across the road and watched from the letter box to see me leave. Then he promptly jumped off the letter box and made his way into the house. How special I felt! Tiger will never be forgotten.

Susan Fyall
Lower Hutt
New Zealand

Jinty goes beyond the call of duty

I am profoundly deaf and my Shetland sheepdog Jinty has been my hearing dog for many years. On several occasions, Jinty has acted above and beyond the call of duty.

The first occasion happened three years ago when Jinty and I had been out all day and returned home. I went into the garden to take some washing in off the line and Jinty followed me out there as she always did. Suddenly she touched my leg to alert me. At first I thought it might be the phone, but when I asked, 'What is it?' Jinty ran across the garden to the boundary fence. As this was unusual behaviour I followed her and looked over the fence, where I saw my elderly neighbour lying on the grass.

I went to fetch help, and we rushed round to help the man, who was shocked and cold. He had been lying there for four hours unable to get up, as he was alone in the house. He was not badly hurt, but without Jinty's help he could have lain there a much longer time, which could have been fatal. He has since moved into a residential home, but has never forgotten how Jinty saved his life.

More recently, Jinty's lifesaving abilities came into play once again. Just after Christmas 2004 I suffered a severe bout of the flu. I got up early in the morning to use the toilet, which is in a small room separate from our bathroom, and, as always, I shut the door.

5

The next thing I knew, I found myself lying wedged between the toilet bowl and the wall, having lost consciousness. I felt too weak to pull myself up, but managed after some effort to slide along the floor and stretch up to open the door. I knew that Jinty would be waiting for me outside the door, and sure enough she was.

My husband Keith also uses hearing aids so I knew there was no use calling to him as he would not have his aids in and wouldn't be able to hear me. When I finally managed to open the door Jinty took one look at me lying there and looked absolutely terrified. I told her to fetch Keith, and that is exactly what she did – not once, but twice, before Keith realised something was wrong and she wasn't just waking him up. We realised that I needed a doctor. When he arrived, he found it hard to believe that Jinty had actually told Keith of my plight.

As if that was not enough, Jinty has also alerted me when Keith was in trouble. Last autumn Keith was trimming the conifer hedge when he slipped off the steps. Jinty was in the garden with him some 85 metres from the house, and I was indoors. Jinty soon sensed that Keith was in trouble. She raced back to the house, alerted me and led me back to the garden where Keith was lying. Luckily Keith was not hurt, just shaken up.

How I would ever manage without her I just don't know. She is such a bright little dog, always willing to please. The more she has to work the happier she seems to be.

Ann Barford
Manningtree, Essex
England

Write to me ... ✉

Ann Barford
c/o Hearing Dogs for Deaf People
The Grange, Wycombe Road
Saunderton, Princes Risborough
Buckinghamshire
HP27 9NS
United Kingdom

Ann and Jinty

Our precious jewel

Our Siamese cat arrived wearing a pink ribbon that accentuated the sapphire blue of her eyes. We called her Bijou – our jewel.

From that moment, Bijou owned everyone and everything, taking over the household as if she knew it was her right. She slept in or on our bed at night and perched high above our heads in the daytime, on any furniture or bench from which she could supervise all our activities. Not that she remained there all the time. A little triangular head pushed itself into whatever we were doing so that she knew exactly what was going on.

When anyone sat down, Bijou was on their knee. However, you were not allowed to read or knit or do anything but pat 'the jewel'.

We were so enchanted with this Siamese cat that we decided to buy another one – one that we could breed from (Bijou had been desexed shortly after we got her).

Instead of exhibiting jealousy when Solange (Sol, for short) arrived, Bijou took a special interest in her. She shepherded her to the toilet, showed her where the best sleeping spots were and curled up with her when she felt lonely.

Once Sol was pregnant, Bijou watched over her like a caring mother, licking her from head to foot and being particularly solicitous as the time approached for the kittens to arrive.

When Sol withdrew into the box under the bed that she had selected for the birth, Bijou crept in with her, licking her face and cuddling close. As each of the kittens was born, Bijou 'top and tailed' it and nudged it towards the 'milk bar'. Between births she tidied up Sol with tender licking.

Bijou remained on duty, minding Sol and the kittens constantly, only popping out to eat and have a short cuddle on someone's lap from time to time as if saying, *I haven't forgotten you, but I have some very important work to do.* When Sol came out briefly to eat or do her business, Bijou curled around the kittens, purring loudly.

As the kittens grew and ventured out into the world Bijou was there, carefully overseeing them and returning lost kittens to their nest if they wandered too far. As they got older, Bijou carried the kittens to the litter tray. If she spotted a kitten squatting with tail aloft on the carpet, she would rush over, cuff it and then drop it unceremoniously in the tray. Bijou's tender care extended to all of Sol's litters. It became the expected behaviour.

Just the same, when we were expecting a baby we wondered how Bijou would react. She carefully inspected all the baby equipment we acquired, just as she inspected any thing or person that came to our home. Bijou never took no for an answer from our friends, some of whom were not cat lovers. Anyone who seemed not to want to be friends was singled out for special treatment: she leaped onto their laps determinedly, purring loudly and offering licks and love bites. Often we had to shut her out of the room, so persistent was she. Then a dainty grey-tipped paw would appear under the door, along with plaintive mews.

At last, baby Glen came and we brought him home. Rather than try to hide the baby from Bijou we laid him carefully on the floor on his bunny rug. She immediately came running over and inspected him from top to toe, sniffing discreetly but not attempting to lick. From then on, Bijou was Glen's guardian, watching over him but never trying to sleep in his crib or get too close.

While Glen slept and I caught up with housework, Bijou perched on the dressing table watching and listening. When he cried, Bijou would hurry to find me and meow until I went to attend to Glen's needs. I never had to worry that I would not hear the baby at night. If I didn't get up immediately when Glen cried, a small body would

9

land on the bed and a grey paw would pat my face with increasing insistence until I staggered out.

As Glen grew older and slept in a bed, Bijou decided it was okay to sleep with him. So she listened to his bedtime story, sitting by his shoulder and looking at the pictures. Then she gave him a little sniff in the ear (which we called a kiss), curled up and went to sleep with him until our bedtime, when she came in to join us.

Glen grew up with Bijou as his closest friend, within reach during all his waking hours. She loved to play with his toys and bat small balls over to him. He loved to feel her plush velvet fur and was gentle with her from the start, never pulling her tail or hurting her in any way. I suppose she might have given him a swat if he had! Once Glen went to school, Bijou would supervise his homework, sitting like a bottle beside him on the desk with her tail wrapped round her feet, nodding and blinking wisely.

Although we had many kittens over time, Bijou, our first Siamese, was our first and dearest love. By the time Glen was a teenager, she was an elderly matron and a bit stiff in the joints. She still liked to curl up on our laps but seldom slept on the bed, preferring to seek the warmth of the heat bank at night.

One night as Glen went to bed, Bijou jumped on the bed and gave him a kiss – something she hadn't done for ages. Then when we went to bed she came and curled up with us. At the time, I thought it was strange as she hadn't done this for so long. Sure enough, the next morning Bijou did not wake up. Our darling, our jewel, had said goodnight forever.

Jan Dunwoodie
Ballarat, Victoria
Australia

Write to me ... ✉
email Jan
jdunwoodie@hotmail.com

The babysitter

The soft-coated wheaten terrier is described by the Canadian Kennel Club as 'an all-purpose working farm dog used for destroying vermin, hunting small animals, herding, and guarding against intruders'. The description should mention that they are also excellent babysitters!

Keeley was four years old when I became pregnant for the first time, and I noticed an immediate change in his behaviour. At first I could not understand why he was so attentive, constantly wanting to be near me, staying close on our walks rather than his normal hunting far afield. After a visit to the doctor, I realised the reason for the change. I also realised the doctor's projected due date was wrong.

Because I listened to Keeley, I was prepared when the baby was born two weeks earlier than the doctor's predicted date. The birth was right on schedule according to Keeley's due date. Positive proof that animals know more than humans.

But there is more to the story than just predicting the birth date.

When I was two or three months pregnant, Keeley started lying outside the bathroom whenever I had a bath or shower. If I accidentally knocked the side of the shower or moved in the tub making it squeak, he would bark until I assured him I was okay.

As the pregnancy progressed and I became larger and more awkward, his barking became louder. To quieten him, I started talking or singing to him when in the bathroom. They were nonsense conversations or silly songs just to reassure Keeley that I was okay. As soon as I was out of the bathroom, Keeley returned to his normal resting place in the living room.

When the baby was born, the 'babysitting' continued in a different way.

11

When a new baby is brought into the house, older dogs will often be jealous. Not so with Keeley: this baby was *his* child. He woke me during the night when the baby cried by sticking his nose on mine – no barking, just snuffling in my face. He stayed near the baby all day, but just out of reach so that little hands could not pull his fur. One experience of tiny fingers pulling on his coat was enough. Visitors were carefully inspected before they were allowed to look at or pick up the baby. This included grandparents, aunts, uncles, nieces, nephews and friends Keeley knew well. No one was allowed near the baby unless he approved.

During the baby's nap time I often worked out in the yard, with Keeley staying either in or near the house. If the baby moved or cried he barked to alert me. I did not need a baby monitor with a wheaten terrier on the job.

Later when my son was walking he liked to play in the yard, quite often by himself when I had inside housework. Keeley again babysat, barking a warning if my son went near the gates or into the shed or garage, or was doing something Keeley felt was not right. Both gates were tied at the top, not to prevent an escaping dog but an escaping child.

Many dog trainers consider terriers to be difficult to train, stubborn and often aggressive. I disagree. Having a wheaten terrier as a babysitter allowed me to do all of the necessary house and yard work.

Betty Hirsekorn
British Columbia
Canada

12

Didi: endless love

'Now, that's what I call a good restaurant!' said Massimo after eating the last piece of his cake. 'Lots of excellent mushrooms and low prices.'

'Low prices above all, that's what you're thinking of!' his brother Enzo, my husband, pointed out.

'True!' Daniela, their sister, got into the conversation. 'Massimo, you're always the same old mean man! Giovanna, how can you be engaged to such a mean person?'

'Well, how can you be engaged to a boy who only thinks of eating?' Massimo replied. 'David, it's a miracle how you succeed in keeping your weight under control!'

'Well, surely you don't mean to say that I chose the wrong restaurant.'

'Of course not, David,' I replied, still savouring the taste of the meal we'd just enjoyed, 'and we're not the only ones to share this opinion. Look at the walls, at all the small pictures of singers, actors, TV stars and football players who've also enjoyed their meals here. There must be hundreds of them! I've spotted all my favourite singers. They've come to this small house up a mountain, near a wood, just to have dinner. There's really something about this place!'

I smiled and looked at the small pictures once again. I started dreaming of the stars who'd eaten in the same restaurant where we were. Little did I know that there was another little beautiful star around, who was much more important than all of them.

We left the room joking and laughing and approached the counter. Nobody was there at that moment, so we had to wait. In front of the counter there were some small tables with four chairs at each. They were there for people to have a quick drink or spend some time playing cards and drinking during the day. Massimo sat on a chair.

13

It was then that we saw a beautiful orange tabby walking towards him. The cat stopped for a moment, then jumped on Massimo's lap and sat down. Massimo was no big cat lover but he agreed that this cat was really beautiful and watched him with curiosity. I couldn't help laughing at his uncertain face. 'You see, Massimo, he's chosen you!'

'You know, Madam' – the restaurant's owner had turned up behind me – 'there's a sad story about this cat.'

'A sad story? Tell us, please, we'd all love to hear it!' And in fact everyone was already listening to the man.

'This cat's name is Didi. You see what a beautiful and quiet cat he is? He's also really clever.

He used to come here with his master. He would follow him to the restaurant's door, then his master would turn towards him and say, "Be a good cat, Didi, wait for me here!" And Didi would sit down outside the restaurant and wait for his master for hours. He never ran away, never followed other cats, he just sat there and waited.

But quite often he was allowed inside. Then he walked straight to his master and jumped on his lap. He could spend hours there while his master played cards, and was never tempted to explore the other rooms or look for something to eat.

Sadly, his master died some months ago. He was in his late fifties and he died suddenly. From then on, Didi has kept coming here every day. He just comes here, sits outside the door and waits.'

'He seems to like my fiancé a lot,' Giovanna said.

'Your fiancé is wearing jeans. His master used to wear jeans and to sit on exactly that chair. That is why each time Didi sees a man wearing jeans and sitting on that chair, he jumps on his lap.'

We all kept silent for a moment, then Massimo spoke softly. 'After hearing this, who could have the heart to stand up and let this cat down?'

I nodded and gave Didi a cuddle. I felt tears in my eyes.

I don't know if Didi's story proves that cats are smart, but surely it proves that they have feelings – strong feelings – and that they miss and never forget the ones they love. A cat's love has to be gained but, once you've gained it, it's forever.

Cristina Giuntini
Prato
Italy

Four heroic dogs in one

My black Labrador Molly was donated to Hearing Dogs for Deaf People. She is now not only my hearing dog but also my indispensable companion.

Before I had Molly, my daughter had to take me out whenever I wanted to leave my home as I suffer from epilepsy. Molly has changed my life completely. I can now go out whenever I want to because Molly will tell me before I have a 'grand mal' fit.

Molly does the work of four dogs.

She is a hearing dog, working to sounds – helping to wake me up and keeping me safe when the fire alarm goes off, among her other sound-work. She also assists me by getting the washing out of the machine and helping me to hang it up, picking things up from the floor, and providing a focal point in front of me which helps my balance.

She is a seizure alert dog, warning me of major fits about 15 minutes before I have one so that I can get to somewhere safe.

She is also a therapy dog. I have to look after her, which encourages me to look after myself properly. She needs exercising and my balance is improved by walking. I get tired when I go shopping, but now I am quite happy to stop for a cup of coffee and a sit down with her, whereas I would feel out of place doing it by myself. I find it easier to go shopping with her. People are much more helpful and willing to accept it when I don't understand what they say. Everyone remembers Molly, so I have to be friendly towards everyone. It is hard to get depressed when you are being friendly.

She is also my friend, and will listen to me when I have a bad night and I want to talk at three in the morning. I would not go back to life without Molly.

I have moved to a houseboat, so Molly has now become the first hearing dog to work and live on a houseboat!

Edward Blacksmith
Lichfield, Staffordshire
England

Write to me …

Edward Blacksmith
PO Box 4154
Lichfield, Staffordshire
WS13 6WZ
United Kingdom

My feline anti-inflammatory

My three-year-old 'naughty tortie' cat likes her routine. I always let her know when it's bedtime, and she happily follows me everywhere until I get into bed and then takes her place at my feet to sleep.

One evening I injured my knee. As always, my cat went to sleep at the end of my bed. During the night I rolled over and groaned in pain. She got up, promptly assessed the situation, then stretched herself down the length of my leg and started purring. This helped in two ways: her body prevented me from rolling over and causing

16

myself more pain, and the vibrations of her purring – similar to those of a machine used during physiotherapy – acted as an anti-inflammatory.

I have since injured my knee a few more times and she always knows when to lie down the length of my leg and start purring! I'm having surgery soon for my knee and wish I could take her to hospital with me.

S Cleland
Auckland
New Zealand

Bear and Tracker – a great team

My mother owns two heroic dogs who work together as a team. Bear is a seven-year-old German shepherd and Tracker a three-year-old Belgian shepherd.

In September 2004 my 84-year-old grandfather went to live with my parents after his wife passed away. He is legally blind because of cataracts and he can only see shadows and figures. He also has mild Parkinson's disease. Sometimes he will black out for a few seconds and fall down – this has happened since he came back from World War II. Whenever it happens, or even if he just misjudges where his chair is and slips a bit, the dogs will run up to him and make sure he's okay.

Every day, he picks up his cane and takes a walk along the path and river front, where there are picnic tables to sit on when he gets tired. The dogs always go with him and my mother will watch the clock to make sure he doesn't go for too long.

This particular day he was out for his usual walk with the dogs when he blacked out and fell. Mom was talking to a friend on the phone, and had a sudden thought that she should go see where her father was. Just as she looked out the window, Tracker came running towards home, alone. Mom asked Tracker, 'Where's Murray?' and he led her along the path.

Mom had been going to head in another direction, but she followed Tracker and, sure enough, he led her to the middle of the trail, where Bear was sitting next to my grandfather, who was trying to get up from his fall.

Tracker always seems to know just what to do in any situation, and Bear is always there to protect others. The way my grandfather tells it, 'Those dogs saved my life.'

Jennifer Carpenter
Fredericton, New Brunswick
Canada

Does your local charity do great work in your community?

Our mission is to help animal charities in their admirable quest to improve the welfare of animals. Do you think your local animal charity does exceptionally good work? We would love hear about it.

The best submission received will be published, with your name, in our quarterly newsletter 'Celebrate Animals'. Animal lovers the world over will then get to see how special your chosen charity is.

Submissions should be 100-200 words. For submission information please go to page 146.

2

Heroic animals find solutions

Heroic Leah (right) and her daughter Kristy

A hairy fish tale!

When I was a kid I had two Cavalier King Charles spaniels, Leah and her daughter Kristy. This breed is well known for its gentle and caring nature, which Leah and Kristy demonstrated on many occasions.

An event that stands out in my memory, however, was the morning when Leah ran frantically out of my bedroom to where I was sitting in the living room. She nuzzled my legs and hands to gain my attention. As I bent down to pat her she ran back towards my bedroom, stopping when I did not follow. She raced back to me and gave me another nudge, so I decided to follow her.

In my bedroom she dropped in front of my dresser and stared at the floor. It was then I noticed that my fish was missing from its tank on the dresser. I got down on my hands and knees beside Leah, and there – covered in carpet fluff and dog hair – was my little fish, still alive but almost unrecognisable. I scooped up my fish and popped him straight back into his tank. He swam off in a flurry, discarding his hairy disguise.

Leah often sat on my bed and entertained herself by watching my little fish swimming around his tank. I am unsure if she had witnessed him flipping out of his tank or had discovered him already on the floor, but either way she had come to his rescue. She looked so relieved when he was back in his watery home, and resumed her front row seat in front of his tank.

Julie Raverty
Echuca, Victoria
Australia

Sheep are not so dumb!

I was busy pruning shrubs beside the driveway, next to the paddock where our small flock of sheep were happily grazing. Lambing had just got under way and I was enjoying the incredibly mild winter and the stress-free production season.

I was about to pack up my tools for the day when I heard a ewe making quite a din. The tone of urgency in her call was increasing as she got nearer to me. When I looked over the hedge, there she was, staring straight at me and obviously rather agitated. At first I couldn't see what she was on about, but then I spotted her lamb, securely wedged between an open gate and the fence. It could not move, and its clever mum had come to me for help.

It was lucky that I was nearby at the right time, as that tiny lamb would surely have died if it had remained there. I moved the gate so that the lamb could get out. Once they were reunited, I enjoyed watching mum and lamb trot off down the paddock. I was even more delighted when mum stopped, turned to me and gave a loud baa as if to say, *Thank you*. Very polite!

Leigh Tuohy
Wellington
New Zealand

Write to me …   ✉
email Leigh
leightuohy@xtra.co.nz

Sam rescued his 'sister'

When I was young we had a Dobermann called Sam. Sam was the same age as me and we even shared a playpen – he was more like my brother than a dog.

When I was eight months old, Sam saved my life. I had a child's walker and was strutting around our house in Wales. I was walking towards my sister, who had just got out of the bath. I was obviously entranced by the bathwater and leaned over to touch it. The walker went in over my head, forcing me under the water. My sister attempted to get me out, but the more she pulled the walker, the further I went under.

Sam went running out of the bathroom and into the kitchen where my mother was. He grabbed her hand and barked. She ignored him

21

until he almost dragged her down the hall. He brought her into the bathroom, where she quickly pulled me out of the water … I was blue and barely breathing.

After that day Sam wouldn't let me out of his sight. It was even said that when I started to have a tantrum he would pull on my nappy, so that I would fall to the ground and start laughing. What a great Dobe (and babysitter, especially when I was in the bath). To this day I still shed a tear when I think of him.

Nadia Crighton
Pymble, New South Wales
Australia

Young Nadia with 'brother' Sam

Not just a ball dog

We acquired Doey, a timid corgi, when she was three and she became a loving and happy dog.

She was about 11 when we got Krystal, a nine-year-old corgi whose elderly owner could no longer take care of her. Although the pair never closely bonded, they respected each other. Krystal was happy anywhere as long as she had a ball. She would push it towards you with her nose and it was your job to kick it away, whereupon she'd chase it and bop it back to you. She would have made a great goalie on a soccer team.

Both dogs slept on mats in our bedroom. One winter night I heard Krystal plonk, plonking down the stairs and out the doggy door. Minutes later, she was back upstairs and standing on her hind legs at my side of the bed, whimpering for my attention. I patted her and told her to go back to bed.

She did so but was soon plonking down the stairs again, then back up and over to my side of the bed and whimpering again. I turned on the light to find that Doey wasn't on her mat. My husband I went downstairs with Krystal, who led us to Doey. She was floundering in the pool.

We assume she'd lost her bearings in the dark, as her senses weren't as sharp as they had once been. We hauled her out, bedraggled and shivering, and ended up drying her with the hairdryer. Krystal got lots of praise for saving Doey's life but she wasn't at all interested. All she wanted to do was – yes, you guessed it – play ball.

Faye North
Katikati
New Zealand

Heroic Krystal (with a ball, of course!) and Doey

She looked after her 'husband'

When I was a boy growing up on a large isolated farm in central Africa, we had two big dogs: a German shepherd male, Skellum, and an English mastiff female, Melody.

There was a lot of bush around and plentiful wild game and, although they knew full well they shouldn't, the dogs would occasionally sneak off to go hunting. One day they didn't return from such a trip. Three days later Melody appeared. She was thin, tired and guilty but fronted up to my father and, by nudging, whining and running back and forth, persuaded him to follow her.

She led him about eight kilometres to where, in thick bush, Skellum was caught in a snare set by an African hunter to catch game. He was dreadfully thirsty, thin and sore from the snare, but survived and fully recovered – thanks to his 'spouse'. She had not only rescued him but had been guarding him from the angry hunter whose trap it was. Later on, they had a litter of 16 beautiful pups.

Angus Faed
Yarloop
Western Australia

Write to me ... ✉

Angus Faed
PO Box 104
Yarloop WA 6218
Australia
or email Angus
tonifaed@hotmail.com

Another 'great team' story

My best buddy Kody was a stray Norwegian forest cat who'd found his way to our 50 acre home. He was very thin when he arrived but regular eating, rest and lots of love soon built Kody back up to the cat he was meant to be.

He quickly assumed the job of guarding the house, and keeping the rodent population under control where needed. Jumping up on my bed early in the morning, he 'talked' and headbutted me out of bed so that I would let him outside and he could perform the job he loved so much. Kody and I always kept a watch over each other throughout the day, visiting each other from time to time for a little talk and for me to scratch him under his chin.

One evening when I was in the workshop a few hundred feet away from the house, Kody came to talk to me. He walked away, turned around, talked to me some more and walked a few more steps. He repeated this a number of times till I figured out that maybe he wanted me to follow him, which I did.

We walked up the small hill to the laneway. I followed him about another 100 feet till he stopped and sat down, looking down the lane and saying nothing more. I looked down the laneway and could see a lump of fur off to one side. I walked towards it to find an animal in distress. About a week earlier, a friend had told me that as he drove up the laneway by the pond he had seen something disappearing into the tall grass – maybe one of our cats – and it appeared to be injured. Since both Kody and his sister Smellycat don't go down to the pond, I'd forgotten about it. Maybe this is what he'd seen.

It was a muskrat in great distress. A muskrat is the size of a small cat and has powerful rear legs. It burrows into the sides of ponds, creating a lot of damage which I continually have to repair.

As I approached, the muskrat pup put up what defences he had left. He could not walk; his front legs were deformed and tucked partially under his chest. His only way of moving was with his head and chest resting on the ground, pushing himself with his rear legs.

He lunged at me feebly while repeatedly chattering his teeth. Big black flies fed from an open wound in the centre of his back. To make matters worse, the wound – a round hole the size of a dime – was infested with maggots. I was amazed that, as bad as this little guy looked, his instinct was still to put on a show to protect himself. Kody sat there watching me, and I understood why he had not dragged this 'catch' back to the garage as he does with his other victims.

I talked to the muskrat to try and calm him down while shooing away the flies. I figured a tick had attached itself to this muskrat and, as is their nature, had worked its way to the back of the muskrat where it had burrowed a hole through the skin and then into the bone of the spine. Once into the spine it destroys the nerves that help the body function. In this case it had damaged the nerves that operated the muskrat's front legs. The tick lays its eggs in the body

Kody got the team together to do what they could

and feeds on the blood till the animal eventually dies. Flies, homing in on this situation, come to feed and breed on the dying animal.

What I was seeing made me cringe but I wanted to help this guy. I got a box and some window screening. I pushed him onto the screening and took him to the laundry tubs in the house, where I tried to wash out the maggots and whatever else might be in the wound.

It seemed the muskrat knew I was trying to help him, for he stopped all his defensive actions against me. After trying to give him water, I put some grass for a bed and some water in the box and took it down to my workshop where it would be out of reach of other animals. I was hoping for a miracle that night.

The next day he did show signs of renewed strength, but by the end of the day things had deteriorated and I felt it best to put the little guy to sleep. Kody came over and watched me as I buried the little box containing the muskrat.

I knew this was just part of the cycle of nature, but I was glad Kody had recognised that this animal was in trouble – just as Kody had been when he first came to my home – and got our team together to do what we could.

In spite of the best efforts of the staff at the Veterinary Emergency Clinic of York Region and Holland Landing Animal Hospital, my best buddy Kody passed away on 24 November 2003. We miss him very much but are very glad he was a part of our lives.

Stan Skurdelis
Sharon, Ontario
Canada

Mack looks out for creatures great and small

Miniature poodle Mack was donated to Hearing Dogs for Deaf People when he was an adult dog. After he had successfully completed his sound-work training he was placed with me. I had recently lost my previous hearing dog Esko, after relying on him for five years to tell me about household sounds such as the telephone, doorbell, alarm clock and smoke alarm. When Mack arrived, I thought it would take a little while for us to build up as strong a bond as I'd had with Esko – but Mack soon proved me wrong.

We were walking into town and had to negotiate a narrow pavement on a blind corner. Just as we were rounding the bend, Mack suddenly gave a loud bark and pulled me sharply into the wall. I was surprised as it was unusual behaviour for Mack, and I was just about to have some stern words with him when I saw a huge articulated lorry mount the pavement about six inches in front of me. With a shock I realised that, had Mack not steered me away so quickly, the lorry would have crushed us both. A lady who had witnessed the whole incident came rushing across the road to see if I was hurt. She told me that she thought we had been hit, and was convinced that Mack had saved my life.

However, it is not only my life that Mack has saved, he looks out for wildlife too. Recently, after a night of particularly high winds, we went into the back garden and found that the bird table had been blown over. Before I could do anything about it Mack raced over to it, then came back to me and touched me. I wasn't taking any notice but he did it several more times, running between the bird table and me, until finally I decided to lift the bird table up. Trapped underneath was a little blue tit that had been feeding when the table had tipped over. Mack had heard it squeaking, and told me about it!

Edna Hind
Cumbria
England

Our clever sheep

Our pet ewe Alice had never had a lamb, as she lived in the small house paddock with the dogs, chooks and occasional calf or pig. There was no way she would associate with the common mob of sheep in the big paddock next door ... or so we thought.

One cold winter's night when she was 11 years old, I was woken by the sound of her frantic calling. This was so unusual that I raced outside and across the frosty yard to see what the trouble was. She had been rushing up and down the fence line as she called, but when she saw me coming she went and stood near her sheltered spot.

29

At her feet was the tiniest blob of yellow newborn lamb I'd ever seen. I believe Alice knew she'd done something important, but had long since lost the instinct that told her what to do next. She did know, however, that if she called me I would solve the problem. If her lamb had been left as he was, he wouldn't have survived until morning.

I quickly cleaned him and got him breathing properly. Alice was rather too low to the ground for a lamb to suckle, even a lamb as small as this one, so I milked her into a jam jar and fed the lamb with a bottle. I continued to bottle-feed Carlos, as I called him, but he learned that he could get extra if he caught his mother lying down, so he grew into a rather large sheep.

Alice lived another three years and Carlos was never far from her. Towards the end, when she would lie down in the long grass and couldn't get up again, Carlos would stand beside her and call until I came to help, just as his mother had done for him on the night he was born.

Viv Atkinson
Waipukurau
New Zealand

A tiny hero

This is a story about one of my parents' many animals. Toots the chihuahua was the last dog they had. She was tiny, but her small size did not stop her from saving my father's life.

It was late at night and my mother was downstairs reading and watching TV. Toots came to her crying. Mom figured that she just wanted to go outside to do her business. However, when they went past the stairs Toots stopped and wouldn't go any further. Mom went back and sat down in the living room. Toots went back into the living room, and the same thing happened about four times until Mom got the picture that Toots wanted to go upstairs to my father.

Mom opened the door for her to go upstairs. Toots ran up the stairs and then ran back to Mom, still crying. Finally, Mom followed Toots to see what the heck she was doing. Mom walked into the bedroom and my father was on the bed having a heart attack.

This happened 18 years ago. Toots passed away two years ago, but my father is still alive and kicking, thanks to Toots!

Bernadette Jordan-Neil
Pasadena, Newfoundland
Canada

Yookie the sharp-eared terrier

It was 8 am and I was trapped in the bathroom. My husband, who wasn't due home until 6 pm, had been fiddling with the lock as he stood outside the bathroom talking to me before he left the house, and now the door was jammed. The window was too small to climb out of and I had no way of contacting anyone.

Then I remembered Grandpa's sharp-eared little terrier Yookie. In desperation, I called him. My voice carried across the garden to next door where the two of them shared a home. Grandpa didn't hear me but, sure enough, Yookie quickly appeared in our backyard looking puzzled at the sight of my face poking out of our tiny bathroom window (I had to balance on the toilet to achieve this feat).

'Go and get Grandpa, Yookie! Get Grandpa!' He looked around once or twice, then shot off. I sat down for what I thought would be a long wait.

31

To my amazement, I soon heard urgent barking and the sound of Grandpa's voice as he approached. 'What's the fuss about, Yookie? Where are you taking me?' It was such a relief to see their two faces looking up at me when I poked my head out of the window. And, although it's true that it was Grandpa who rescued me from the bathroom, we were all so amazed at Yookie's intelligent response to my call for help that he became a legend in our family overnight.

Penny Auburn
Newport, New South Wales
Australia

Sure, animals are smart, but do you know a smart person?

Do you know a special person who will do just about anything to help animals – a true hero of the human species? Someone who has made a real difference to animals' lives? We'd love to hear about them.

The best submission received will be published, with your name, in our quarterly newsletter 'Celebrate Animals'. Animal lovers the world over will then find out how special this person is.

Submissions should be 100-200 words. For submission information please go to page 146.

3

Heroic animals take care of each other

Shadow's assistant

We have two Border collie/kelpie dogs named Shadow (13 years old) and Phoebe (seven years old).

Shadow is still feisty and very much the 'top dog', but she is now arthritic and has lost most of her hearing and sight. Phoebe has become her eyes and ears.

When my husband arrives home from work and Shadow has not heard his car in the drive, Phoebe runs to Shadow to tell her he is home by licking her face and then running to the gate, with Shadow running along behind her. Likewise, if it is time for them to go outside and Shadow is sound asleep, Phoebe runs to tell Shadow (again by licking her face) that it is time to go out to the toilet, and Shadow jumps up and follows her outside.

This is not something we taught them, it's just something they instinctively worked out for themselves, but we always tell Phoebe she is a 'good girl' when she has done her job.

Sue Curran
Mt Torrens
South Australia

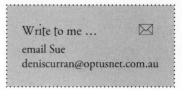

Write to me ... ✉
email Sue
deniscurran@optusnet.com.au

Doodah the nurse

I have always been surrounded by animals. I have never lived in a house that didn't have at least a cat to go with it. Often this translated to a few cats, a dog, a troop of hens, lambs, a calf, ducks, Canada geese, hedgehogs, rabbits, fish – and a partridge in a pear tree.

Growing up with animals is a truly extraordinary experience. How many people could say they'd had a bath with 12 ducklings? Or made friends with a seal? I feel special because of it. I have a thousand stories to share, a thousand memories – and they all seem to start and end with my father Bill.

One of Bill's rescued animals was a dog that he saved from her master. The story goes that this poor little puppy's master had treated her very badly. I only found out later how badly and I won't go into it, except to say that she never chased a stick in her life, and it was a long time before she would even come into the house or trust men without beards. My father, needless to say, has a beard you could lose mice in.

The dog's master's wife had begged us to help the dog, so we did. We gave her a home, we gave her love and slowly she came out of her shell. She was a cross between a Labrador, a greyhound and a Dobermann (we think), and as black as the ace of spades. Her name had been Shebah but we called her Doodah, firstly because she ran like a racehorse, and secondly because my little brother couldn't say her name and the closest he could get was 'Deedah'.

Doodah was a lovely dog, with big brown eyes that always looked depressed, even when she wasn't. She was also gentle. Having grown up with the cats, she never chased a single one in her life. She let babies pull her fur, kittens chew her ears, birds dive-bomb her – all with a look of long-suffering melancholy. And she never barked, not once.

Doodah's best friend was one of our cats, CT (short for Cottontail). Bill had rescued CT along with his siblings, FM (Flopsy Mopsy) and Peter, after finding them in a sack in a sewer. Sadly, when he was about six years old, CT got cancer in the base of his tail. It was a strange thing – nobody knew how it had happened, and the cancer spread up through his spine in just a week. What was even stranger, though, was what happened next.

You might not believe me, but I swear this is the truth, though I've never heard or seen the like of it since. As the disease progressed, CT lost the use of his back legs, so Doodah took it upon herself to help him go to the toilet. She would pick him up in her mouth and carry him outside. Then she'd dig a little hole for him, put him over it and wait for him to do his business. When he'd finished, she'd fill in the hole and clean him before picking him up again, carrying him back into the house and laying him on the couch.

She did this about three times a day and none of us could figure out how she knew just when he needed to go, but she did. She would lie by the couch, looking sad, and then she'd just raise her head and look at him – that's all we knew. I will never forget that – a silly old mongrel dog, going grey around the muzzle, carrying a full-grown cat in her mouth. Making his life just that little bit easier before he died.

Arja Hone
Wellington
New Zealand

Ashley remembered her babies

Many people think that cows don't remember their calves and that they don't mind very much when their babies are taken away from them at just a few days old, but I know differently.

One of my uncle's dairy cows, Ashley, was special to us because she had been a Calf Club calf (a pet calf). Because she was a dairy cow, Ashley's calves were taken off her at about two days old. Every year, Ashley and her new calf would be taken to the cowshed, where the calf was taken from her and put in a pen with the other calves.

During her time as a dairy cow, Ashley had ten calves. Two of them were kept to join the dairy cow herd when they grew up. Just like Ashley's other calves, they were taken away from her at about two days old. Ashley did not see them again until they joined the herd as two-year-olds.

My uncle thought it was a little strange when Ashley started spending time in the paddock with the first of her calves to join the herd. Two years later, when another of her calves came into the herd, you would go into the shed at milking time and see the three of them lined up, one after the other, in the bails. Clearly, Ashley remembered her calves.

Ashley was kept in the herd for much longer than most cows because I wouldn't let my uncle sell her. Eventually she was too old to have any more calves, so at age 13 she came to live at our farm. To everyone's surprise, Ashley got pregnant again. We were concerned because of her age, but she successfully had a little calf we called Emily.

Ashley had much more milk than tiny Emily could drink, so we decided to take her to our retired cowshed to milk her and make her more comfortable. Ashley made it clear that she did not want to go to the shed – she was a very big Friesian cow, so we had to push and

Ashley with her beloved calf Emily

shove her. Eventually, we got her in the shed and milked her. When we put her back in the paddock she just stood by the gate looking forlorn.

After about an hour of Ashley standing there, I wondered whether she thought we'd taken Emily away. Emily was lying in the long grass, so Ashley wouldn't have been able to see her from where she was standing. I went into the paddock and lifted Emily up onto her feet, then I called to Ashley to have a look. Ashley gave out a loud moo, then ran over to Emily and started sniffing and licking her. She obviously thought that, since she had been into the cowshed, Emily had been taken away from her, just like all the other calves she had had.

37

Ashley died the winter that Emily turned one. Emily was with her on the night she died. Ashley's last year was her best as she finally got to keep one of her babies, and I know she died a happy cow.

Gina Sturkenboom
Hamilton
New Zealand

Write to me ... ✉
email Gina
gas4@waikato.ac.nz

Jack's special gift to a blind stranger

We live on a farm with traditional working dogs. One in particular, Jack, is the 'head dog'.

One day a friend came to stay to help build an addition to our hayshed. He brought with him a blind Labrador, Jess, whom he was looking after while Jess's mistress was on holiday. When the men had gone to work on the farm, I looked at the bewildered Jess and decided to take him for a walk. As I passed our dog kennels the dogs started barking. Although I didn't think it wise for the dogs to accompany us on our walk, for some unknown reason I let them all off.

After the usual sniffing and introductions we all started off for a walk through the forest. The dogs ran off ahead – except, unusually, Jack. Now, Jack is a dominant, selfish, jealous, one-man dog who always has to be ahead of the others. But this time he remained back with me and walked slightly ahead of Jess, close enough that he was touching him.

We reached a large clearing and Jack made a most unusual noise. I decided (again, for some unknown reason) to let Jess off the lead.

Jack nudged Jess away from me and appeared to be guiding him around the clearing. Before long they were cantering together, with Jack slightly ahead but still touching Jess. The other dogs, who loved to play, remained some distance away and only came when I whistled that it was time to head home. On our walk back through the forest I didn't put the lead back on Jess; instead, he walked ahead of me with his tail wagging and Jack beside him.

When the men returned home that night I told them what had happened. My husband couldn't believe that Jack would do anything for anyone, let alone another dog (except maybe a bitch). Our friend was very happy that Jess had been able to run, because since he had lost his sight he never went anywhere without someone beside him and he only ever walked.

A week later we were told that Jess had been killed in a motor accident. I took heart in the fact that he had been given the chance to once more run freely without fear – all because Jack, for the first time in his life, did a caring act for a not-so-able dog he'd never met before.

Helen Scully
Bulls
New Zealand

Titus and Asterix

Titus was a lilac point Siamese who came to us as a three-month-old kitten. Shy and timid when he first arrived, he grew up to be confident and independent, and established himself as leader of the local feline gang. But he was gentle by nature, and it was gentleness that led to his most heroic act.

Kind-hearted Titus

He was very territorial and would suffer no interlopers in his garden, but one winter night he came in through his private entrance followed by a black cat we had never seen before. Not only was the newcomer ushered in by Titus, but he was invited to join him on his storage radiator, an old-fashioned wide-topped affair kept intentionally at a low heat for him to sleep on. The two cats – black and white – curled up together, and the newcomer was always welcome in the house from that day on.

Naturally we set out to trace the black cat's owners, and found them in a cottage at the far side of the allotments abutting our garden. They told us that his name was Asterix and they had taken him in as a stray kitten, although he was so weak and ill they had doubted his chances of survival. Then, out of the blue, in walked a strange Siamese (our Titus) who proceeded to tend to the sick kitten, washing him and settling down to sleep beside him. Asterix survived, and the two cats were bosom friends from that day on.

It was not until the onset of winter that Titus brought his friend home to the warmest spot he knew. By one kindly act, he had brought us another lovely cat – whom he never ceased to groom and care for – and a pair of good new human friends.

Patricia Johnson
Brentwood, Essex
England

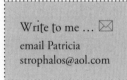

Write to me … ✉
email Patricia
strophalos@aol.com

One of the family

Deefa was a King Charles spaniel, and Jazz the Siamese cat was her friend. They played together, slept together and were inseparable. However, it was a case of 'two's company', and the common grey tabby cat Mist was the outsider. The only time she was accepted by them as part of the family was when they all got together in the lounge room at night.

My daughter Christine arrived home one day to find that both Deefa and Mist had gone missing. Although Mist often wandered off by herself, Deefa never strayed so this was unusual.

Christine searched high and low over the two acre block. The grass was long and she couldn't see or hear anything. At last she found the two together, Mist stretched out rigid and cold on the ground. Beside her stood Deefa, frantically licking the tabby all over, not stopping even when Christine arrived.

My granddaughter Gemma arrived home from school. She and Christine took Mist to the local vet, who said she'd been bitten by a snake. Deefa may not have had much time for Mist in the past, but her non-stop licking had kept the cat's circulation going until help arrived.

With the help of some fairly expensive veterinary treatment, Mist lived. Christine and her husband Ian did not begrudge the expense. After all, she was one of the family.

Joan Hutchison
Ringwood, Victoria
Australia

The pony and the ram

We finally arrived at our new home – a derelict croft on the remote Shetland Islands – armed with enthusiasm, itchy feet and enough practical self-sufficiency books to deal with any eventuality. Well, almost.

Those rare days off that could be spared from refurbishing the cottage we spent exploring all the new places that were to be found on the map. And there were 3000 miles of coastline to choose from …

Which was how, one day early on in our exploring, we came to be at Jarlshof. Sitting at the southern tip of the Shetland mainland, Jarlshof is one of the best examples of pre-Viking settlements to be found in northern Europe. Planted like a cloven hoofprint between the towering cliffs of Sumburgh Head and Fitful Head, on a summer's day the view of the sea is stunning … but not on this one. Three days of continuous rain had put paid to all outside work on the house, and I thought that for once it would be good to look around somewhere that was in even worse shape than our new home. Jarlshof, a ruin of stone and earthworks, seemed ideal.

We parked the car and made our way round to the entrance on a path running between a high wall and a paddock. The only other occupants on that miserable day were two local residents: a Shetland pony and a huge ram. Even to my untrained eye, it was immediately apparent that something was very wrong. The ram, with his magnificent head of horns, was lying on his side gasping and struggling for breath as the pony stood over him.

For some reason, my first thought was that the ram had butted the pony (well, isn't that what they do with their horns?) and the pony, like any haughty stallion, had reared up and delivered a mighty kick. This idea was further reinforced when the stallion began to reach down and bite his adversary. I hurried over to see what could be done from behind the safety of the wooden fence.

When I got there, things appeared quite different. For one thing, it was obvious that the ram was ancient. His glassy eyes were almost straining out of their sockets, and his black spindly legs kicked

43

feebly as the last of his strength ebbed away. Mentally, I worked at a furious pace. I was a walking encyclopaedia of practical self-sufficiency and animal husbandry – surely I had the answer to his ailment somewhere? But my knowledge of crop rotation, treatment of scaly leg and emergency plumbing repairs wouldn't help here …

And then, as I sat there feeling futile, I realised something incredible. The pony, rather than biting the old ram, was actually trying to help his poor friend to stand up. Gently but firmly, he had been taking mouthfuls of that grey oily fleece and using all his strength to get the ram upright. We continued to watch in admiration as he tried bravely, but in vain, to haul the old fellow up. But some last nagging doubt, welling up from *Black's Veterinary Dictionary*, made me feel that the ram's time was near. I dashed through the entrance and into Jarlshof, where the old custodian was sitting in his little booth.

'You have to come quickly, I think your ram is dying,' I panted, dripping rain and rapid explanations over his nice dry floor.

'Why, yun old ram is maybe the better part of 12 year old, an' he's no' been shorn for maist 'o them. His coat's just waterlogged you see, an' he canna get up.'

Sheepishly (yes, I think that's the only word – sheepishly), I trudged back outside and surveyed the situation with new eyes. The pony was still tugging away persistently, but moved off when I vaulted the fence – now strangely fearless and closer than ever before to both stallions and sheep with big horns. And when, after much struggle, I eventually succeeded in pulling the old ram to his feet, he simply shook out half his weight in water and plodded over to his friend.

I think that was the first time part of me really felt connected to the land and this whole self-sufficiency thing. But the pony, watching me from a safe distance, wasn't fooled: his patient look told me I wasn't pulling the wool over anyone's eyes …

Gary Wright
London
England

Happiness times five

I have always liked cats. As a child I used to bring cats home, whether they were stray ones or just someone's cat out for a walk.

Once, when I was 13, I was walking home from our school bus stop and my eyes fell upon a dark grey tabby cat hidden behind a tuft of grass alongside the country road. I called, 'Hi, kitty', and the cat, forgetting all about hiding, pounced out onto the road and trotted towards me, purring all the while as if we were old friends. 'Well, kitty,' I said, 'I can take you home, but you must stay in the barn, because you know Mom's rules about animals in her house.' Having made a nice bed of hay for my new tenant, I hurried off to the house for dinner.

I had put my school books and lunch bucket away and was just beginning to tell Mom and Dad how I had found a stray cat and had brought it home and how it would stay at the barn, when we heard a meow at the back door. Dad opened the door and in trotted my new friend. She looked up at Dad and said *Meow* as a thank you and went to the chair nearest the cook stove, hopped up on it, washed

45

her face with her paws and purred the most contented purr I had ever heard. She lay down, curled her long slender tail around her soft furry body and sang herself to sleep. She won everyone over with her ladylike performance, and even Mom loosened the rules about animals in the house.

We learned shortly afterwards to whom the cat belonged but her owner said that, since I loved her so much, I could keep her for a while.

During that little while, the cat became the mother of five lovely kittens. They were the liveliest little balls of fur one would ever want to see. They gave us many hours of entertainment as we watched them progress from one stage to the next – whether it was wrestling with one another, trying to run across a slippery waxed floor or climbing the stairs for the first time.

Meanwhile, the real owner said she would like her cat back as soon as the kittens were old enough to survive without their mother. So when the day arrived I picked up the mother cat, told her to say goodbye to her babies and headed off down the road on the three-quarter mile hike to her rightful owner.

The next afternoon the cat returned to the farm once more. She did not come into the house but gazed through the farmhouse screen door at her kittens wrestling on the kitchen floor. They were so busy playing they didn't even see her, nor did she try to get their attention in any way. After watching for a few minutes and satisfying herself that her babies were all right, she slowly turned and once more headed down the country road to her rightful owner – this time, alone.

Helen French
Newmarket, Ontario
Canada

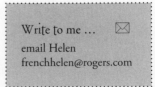

Write to me …

email Helen
frenchhelen@rogers.com

The little goat who could

Toegy was our pet Toggenburg goat. He had been a gift from a friend when he was just a kid, and over the years he became a constant companion and part of our family.

My husband Bob and I operated a training and show stable for Arabian horses in Langley, British Columbia. Toegy was our barn-yard mascot and had the full run of our facility.

He spent his days getting into everything – dumping buckets of grain, turning on taps, racing through the barns, and exercising an evil sense of humour where pesky children or nervous ladies were concerned. He loved to run along the top of our wooden rail fences when the horses ran in their paddocks, and he was always ready for a nuzzle with a horse or a cuddle with one of the dogs.

Toegy also had a strong sense of duty, and he especially liked to stand beside my husband when Bob was working with young horses – putting them through their paces on the lunge line, walking behind them as he taught them to drive in harness or teaching riders to handle their mounts. If goats could talk, I am sure Toegy would have been quite capable of giving riding lessons himself after all the training he watched while standing beside Bob over the years.

During this time we had a very beautiful and valuable stallion in our stable called Tutankhamen. He was nicknamed 'Tut', but I am sure he would have preferred the full moniker as he took his ancestral lineage quite seriously and seemed to consider himself to be the most beautiful horse in the world. Being so important he had little time for the other animals that walked the Earth with him. His aloofness was ever present: he chased the dogs, kicked at the cats and, should the barnyard goat venture into his paddock, was quick to place a well-aimed nip on Toegy's hindquarters, sending him smartly on his way.

47

Toegy learned that being in the vicinity of Tut was not a safe place to be and, after a few painful bites to his posterior, decided he would cease and desist all association with the stallion.

For some reason Tut became very ill one day. He wouldn't eat or drink and was very lethargic and uninterested in his surroundings. Our veterinarian was unable to find any cause for the illness, but treated the horse for all the possible causes that he could think of.

Tut, however, got no better. In fact, he became sicker and weaker. No matter what we did to help him it was to no avail. When he finally gave up the fight and lay down in the centre of our indoor arena, we thought that this was the end of the beautiful stallion and now he was just waiting to die. Toegy had other ideas.

The little goat who Tut had treated so meanly went out into the arena and lay down with his back against Tut's. He stayed beside that stallion for 36 hours, refusing to leave the suffering horse. Even when it was time for his dinner, Toegy remained on his quiet vigil, ignoring all our attempts to coax him away from the stallion's side.

The little goat who could, did! Toegy, in his own way, was supplying support for the ailing Tut – support that only another animal could provide. All of the medications and treatments could not give Tut the healing bedside manner and companionship that Toegy somehow knew he required.

We watched the two, side by side in quiet companionship for those 36 hours, until Tut slowly rose to his feet and shook the dirt from his coat. Then Toegy also stood up, and walked out of the arena to find Bob and see what he was up to with the horses.

Tut steadily improved and was himself again within a few days, strutting about importantly and showing no signs of the battle he had not fought alone.

Toegy never did return to the stallion. Somehow he knew that his job was done – his caring had provided the spark that gave Tut the will to live – and that he was no longer needed.

In his own way he became a hero and was indeed 'smarter than Jack'.

Jill Hayward
Louis Creek, British Columbia
Canada

A truly beautiful soul

My parents have bred Afghan hounds for over 30 years, since their inception as the 'in vogue' breed of the '70s. At one time they had two bitches, Honeysuckle and Roses.

Honey was heavily pregnant, her belly hanging low and her breathing quite laboured. We were slightly worried about her breathing, but since a large litter can place pressure on the internal organs and squash them up against the lungs, we passed it off as normal. She was also losing weight. Once again, not that unusual when the body is carrying so many little ones, placing additional demands on calcium and energy.

All went as expected and, at around day 63, Honey went into labour in the heated whelping box and delivered 12 extraordinarily healthy and large puppies – all fat-bodied with stubby limbs, yelping their little puppy yelps and blindly seeking warmth. However, Honey was still showing signs of labour and was rapidly becoming exhausted. My parents called the emergency vet, who promptly arrived, established that the remaining puppy was in the breech

49

position and, after anaesthetising Honey, set about performing a Caesarean.

He then noticed something unusual about Honey's breathing. The right side of her chest wasn't moving at all when she exhaled. After a little exploration he discovered her to be riddled with cancer. He advised that she should be allowed to awaken from the anaesthetic as it was important that she feed her puppies – particularly the first milk, which contains the immunity-providing colostrum. Honey had shown no signs of suffering prior to this, so my parents agreed and left her to recover with her babies under the warmth of the heat lamp.

Honey passed away in the early hours of the morning. What to do? Raising a litter of 13 puppies by hand was an onerous task, requiring bottle-feeding with specially formulated milk every four hours, toileting of the puppies, and a good four solid weeks of shift work and insomnia. Then my parents had an idea: Rosie. Rosie was particularly gentle and maternally orientated and had raised several fine litters with tireless patience and pride. Could she be the orphaned puppies' mother?

Dad introduced the puppies to Rosie. Rosie sniffed them, haltingly rolling them over with her nose. Then she turned and walked away. It looked like hand-raising would be necessary after all.

Then my father had another idea. He carefully washed all 13 puppies in warm water, lathering their coats in sweetly fragranced shampoo and conditioner, then towel-dried them. Rosie was brought in for a second inspection. Again, she sniffed each puppy and rolled them over, then hesitated, seeming to think things over. A moment later she climbed into the whelping box, carefully winding her way around the puppies and situating herself with them around her belly.

Rosie kept those puppies warm, cleaned them after they were bottle-fed, and took on the countenance of an extremely proud mother. *Just look at my babies!* Even more miraculously, Rosie started to produce milk herself and managed to feed all of those puppies, despite her not being pregnant or even in season.

Rosie's new puppies grew fast and furiously. In just over a week, their little eyes, previously glued shut, had opened to the world. Days later, they were taking their first steps, dragging their little bottoms behind them like wheelbarrows in reverse. Then came the teeth. Puppies are little vampires, with needles for teeth. Everything and anything of three dimensions was fodder for chewing, and Rosie's ears – hanging elegant and long with their pale gold locks – were first choice. Rosie endured this, never once snapping at the puppies, who hung like grotesque decorations from her lovely coat. This was the stuff of real motherhood!

The puppies graduated to eating meat from a big bowl, though still returned to torment their indefatigable mother. She licked them clean, though this must have been becoming an arduous task. Thirteen big puppies cavorting, romping, somersaulting over each other, then settling back with their mum after expending that puppy energy. Rosie was looking tired. Tired, but grimly determined.

Puppies were now beginning to leave as prospective owners arrived and took them home. Rosie did not seem to mind, or even notice that her brood was diminishing. There was no loss in overall energy – one puppy would leave, and the others would grow stronger still, demanding more and more of their mother. They were growing so quickly that they were almost the same height and stature as Rosie, though without the magnificent long coat. No, theirs was the ungainly shag rug of a house from the '70s – quite fitting, given the golden age of their breed. Although they were ungainly and long-limbed teenagers, with teenagers' energy, they still hung off Rosie's ears and she never tired of it.

Rosie successfully raised all of her puppies. My parents kept two of them to show. These two were particularly vocal, mischievous and attention-seeking. They would hang off Rosie's ears, their baby teeth well and truly uprooted, their adult set sparkling – razor sharp and snappish.

These days, Rosie is not so mobile as she's developed arthritis in her shoulder but, although the flesh may weaken, the spirit is willing … though her main wish now is to come up to the house, lie down in front of the fire, wag her tail to acknowledge your presence and lift her head if the slightest suspicion of chicken is insinuated. However, she stays firmly rooted.

A proud mother, a generous and loving creature, Rosie is truly a beautiful soul.

Dr Rebbecca Wilcox
Mordialloc, Victoria
Australia

Write to me … ✉
Dr Rebbecca Wilcox BVSc BAnSci
PO Box 155
Greensborough VIC 3088
Australia

4

Heroic animals lend a paw

Faye made my job much easier

In my younger days, I worked as a shepherd in preparation for getting my own sheep farm. I had a very good, strong eye-heading bitch called Faye. I always took her with me on my lambing beat, during which I often had to assist a cast sheep to get back on its feet. For non-farming folk, a sheep becomes cast if it has lain for too long on one side. The usual way to help a cast sheep get back up was to just roll it over on its other side until its legs regained mobility, which could sometimes takes a while.

One day, however, Faye went over to a cast sheep before I could get to it. She stood behind it, leaned over it, then grabbed its belly wool and pulled it over on its other side – all without my help. Imagine my surprise and pleasure, as I had never taught her to do anything like that. She saved me a lot of time and effort from then on.

Tim Suckling
Katikati
New Zealand

Oscar understood my silent plea

I once had two cats that went by the names of Crystal and Oscar. They were from the same litter and at this point in time were two and a half years old. Both were black and white and very small for their age.

One day Crystal went out to play and didn't come back that night. As she often slept outside this didn't worry us much. We had recently moved to a new house, and we assumed that she would spend the night exploring and then come back the next day.

However, there was no sign of her when morning came and, naturally, we became a little worried. Thinking that we would search for her that night if she didn't show up during the day, we went about our daily activities as per usual.

After we got back we made a quick search inside, calling for Crystal, but she did not appear. We ran out the double doors onto the veranda, constantly calling her name. Still she did not turn up. Crystal had never been missing for more than a day before. I had this horrible image of our poor girl lost in some dark alley, or trapped inside somebody's cold garage. I went to bed heartbroken.

The next day we quickly searched the house and then ran out to look for her. By now we were quite panicked as it was the third day that she had been missing. We discussed the idea of putting up flyers on posts, or going door to door to ask the neighbours if they had seen her. I silently prayed that it would not have to come to that.

You may think this story is just about my gorgeous kitty going missing, because up until now it has been. But this is where my genius cat Oscar comes in.

The next day, Saturday, I woke up at eight and went into the lounge where both cats usually slept. Before I went outside to search for Crystal I glanced at Oscar, who was watching me out of the corners of his beady eyes. I gave him a pleading look, and it was then that he seemed to understand the gravity of the situation. He stared at me with his eyes wide open – it was a look that I will never forget. Then he ran outside.

Ten minutes crawled slowly by. Suddenly I heard a faint meow. I opened the double doors and saw Oscar forcing Crystal up the wooden steps, using his nose to push her. He was the family hero, earning himself a lot of pampering!

Sadly my beloved Oscar got very sick and we had to put him to sleep. I will always remember Oscar, a cat with huge personality.

Maddi Empson
Wellington
New Zealand

Obedient Maxwell earns his keep

Maxwell the golden Labrador had already been out for his morning run with his mum and was snoozing happily on the spare bed in the morning sun. My partner Quentin had gone to clear the mail, and found himself locked outside when the front door slammed shut. Quentin went to find the spare key but, unfortunately, I had used it two days earlier and had not yet replaced it. So there was Quentin, stuck outside, peering through the sun porch windows at Maxwell fast asleep on the bed in the sun. What a quandary! However, Quentin had an idea. That rascal dog was going to earn his keep.

As luck would have it, we had recently removed the wall between the sun porch and the spare room where Max was sleeping, and there was a cat door installed in the sun porch door by the previous owners. So there was Quentin, lying on the front porch with his head through the cat door, calling Max to wake him up from his

55

sleep. Max, being the obedient dog that he is, came bounding off the bed and over to the cat door. Quentin then asked Maxwell to retrieve 'the phone, the phone, Max!' that was sitting next to the bed. Maxwell obliged by bringing the phone. I then got a phone call at work from a very proud dad and, other than me being told off for not replacing the spare key, everyone was in good spirits.

There was still one problem, though – the house keys! But we had a plan. Quentin called Maxwell back to the cat door and told him to go to 'the front door, the front door, Max!' Maxwell once again obliged. Once there, Quentin yelled through the front door to get 'the keys, Max, the keys!' which were sitting on the shelf next to the front door. It took several attempts and some scratches on the door and side wall, but a few moments later, much to his delight, Quentin heard the clinking of keys. Maxwell then trotted back to the cat door, where a very relieved Quentin was eagerly waiting and calling him, and dropped the keys into Quentin's hand.

Let's just say that we ran out of Maxwell's treats that day!

Janine Campbell
Wellington
New Zealand

Rhett the superdog

Before we emigrated to Australia 25 years ago we needed to sell our house in Cape Town, South Africa. We had three weekends of open inspections, during which our first real estate agent insisted that we send our dog Rhett away (temporarily) because we did not have a kennel we could lock him up in.

The next agent allowed us to keep Rhett in the garden. He was a large, super-good-looking Irish setter who was both superfriendly and superintelligent.

The first couple that arrived that Saturday afternoon had two lovely young children with them. Rhett approached the kids, happily nuzzled them and then led them upstairs to the bedrooms.

Just ten minutes later, their parents asked us, 'If you are emigrating, may we buy the dog with the house?'

So they did both, which proved that Rhett was also a supersalesman.

Graynom Brown
Vaucluse, New South Wales
Australia

Write to me ... ✉
Graynom Brown
11-23 Diamond Bay Road
Vaucluse NSW 2030
Australia

Wipe your feet!

We were living in Winnipeg, Manitoba. The soil is the consistency of gumbo, so I taught our Scottie dog Angus to wipe his feet on the doormat before entering the house. He would stand there on the mat dragging his feet back and forth, trying to remove all trace of the sticky soil.

Joycelyn M Head
Calgary, Alberta
Canada

Write to me ... ✉
Joycelyn Head
302-20 Promenade Pk SE
Calgary AB T2Z 4A5
Canada

Spirited Tse Yau

My helpful hearing cat

The sun was shining – quite a bonus as it was the second week of July.

I had some seedling tomatoes, which were really far too early since winter had only just started, with several hard frosts. I was keen to put them out in my glasshouse and nurture them until spring.

The glasshouse was messy, with the remains of the summer's spider webs and the general clutter of a busy season. A spring clean

– emptying out everything and an all-over brush with the hose – seemed the only thing to do.

My cat Tse Yau (Chinese for 'freedom'), a five-month-old farm tabby of wild parentage, was with me. As usual she didn't want to miss anything and was fossicking under, behind and into everything.

I was busy washing out pots when the cat suddenly dashed out of the glasshouse, ran round me once and tore off towards the house. She looked back to see if I was following and dashed back to repeat a quick circuit of me, then made another dash towards the house. At first I couldn't make out what was happening, but then I could hear the faint sound of a phone ringing – was it ours? It was, and to the delight of the cat I followed in hot pursuit.

The young cat already recognised the tone of our phone compared with that of our neighbours, and had also learned that I always stopped whatever I was doing and rushed to the phone when it rang.

Talk about hearing dogs – I've got a 'hearing cat'!

POSTSCRIPT: Sadly, a few months after this story was written, our much loved Tse Yau was killed on the road aged only ten months. She couldn't resist visiting her two cat friends who lived at the corner section opposite us. Her price for freedom and our great loss; she definitely had 'personality plus'.

Faye Ross
Ngatea, Hauraki Plains
New Zealand

In the care of Rommell

Quite a few years ago my family and I owned a male German shepherd called Rommell and a female tortoiseshell cat called Annie. The two had grown up together and they got along really well.

A couple of weeks after Annie had a litter of kittens she decided to go walkabout. We were really worried about her and also about the kittens. They had started to cry and we were concerned about what to do. We knew we could give them special milk if we had to, but they needed constant supervision. Who would watch over them?

Rommell watched us as we discussed the problem and he seemed very curious about the crying kittens. We knew he would never hurt the kittens as he was such a gentle giant, so we left him in the garage with them while my parents, sisters and I went into the kitchen to work out a kitten-watching roster and the other family members went out looking for Annie.

When we went back out to the garage we found that the kittens were missing from their box. We were very worried and confused. Then we heard Rommell moving around in our old broken-down van. The side door of the van was always left open as Rommell liked to sleep in it. We went over to the van as fast as we could. I remember thinking, 'Oh no, what has he done to the poor kittens!' We looked in and there was Rommell happily lying down while the kittens crawled all over him. They weren't crying but did appear to be looking for milk, so my mum drove to the local vet and came back shortly afterwards with some kitten formula.

While my mum and sisters fed the kittens, I took Rommell and told him to find Annie. He looked at me several times and then sniffed around the yard before heading down towards some bush. I followed him.

After we had been walking for about five minutes, he suddenly stopped and started to bark. When I caught up to him, he walked in front of me and stopped again. I looked down and realised there was a large hole in the ground. I couldn't see very well as it was getting dark, but I could hear meowing coming from the hole.

I didn't know what to do, so I took my jumper off, lay down on the ground and placed the jumper over the edge of the hole. I called out to Annie and kept talking to her, trying to encourage her to somehow grab the jumper. It didn't work, so I found a long branch and tried the same thing.

Finally, I heard Annie trying to scramble up the branch. When I felt her weight on the branch I dragged it up slowly. Rommell grabbed hold of the branch too and tried to help me pull it back up. We got the branch up and there was Annie hanging on for dear life. I took Annie back home and we took her straight to the vet. It looked like a dog had attacked her as she had quite a few cuts here and there. The vet stitched her up, but we weren't allowed to put her with the kittens for some time.

We solved the problem of the kittens missing their mother by placing Annie in a large cage in the van. Rommell automatically lay down with the kittens. We took care of feeding them, and Rommell gave them company and protection until Annie was well enough to take over.

My parents decided Annie wouldn't have any more kittens and she was desexed a month later. Annie and Rommell remained great mates for many years.

Simone Polovich
Burpengary, Queensland
Australia

Jerry (in front) and friend Sheha the Second outside with the hens

A great helper and protector

Living on half an acre, we had 12 chooks roaming free in the backyard. It was quite a chore to rummage around the bushes and trees searching for the eggs they had laid each day.

As collecting eggs became part of our daily routine Jerry, our Jack Russell, saw it as an opportunity to interact with us and have some fun. When we stepped out into the yard at the same time each day, he would scurry around looking under bushes and trees. When he found some eggs, he would pick them up ever so carefully in his mouth and excitedly run back and drop each one into my palm in perfect condition, without any cracks. He would then rush back out to collect more eggs.

Not only was he a great help around the yard, he also made sure we didn't leave behind any hidden eggs.

Jerry is also my close guardian who protects me from my greatest fear – spiders!

At one stage we were getting quite a few big black spiders in our house, and when I saw one I would scream. Jerry quickly realised spiders were not one of my favourite things. He got so used to me shrieking that, when I walked into my study where the spiders would normally be, he would dash into the room in front of me and cautiously look up at the ceiling and along the walls, scanning the room for spiders. Funnily enough, each time he did this there were none in sight! I always wonder, though, if there had been one what he would have done. Nevertheless, he was there as my protector and calmed me down. I am grateful to him as he has put a little humour into my fear.

Madeline Stathopoulos
Avonsleigh, Victoria
Australia

Your say . . .

Here at SMARTER than JACK we love reading the mail we receive from people who have been involved with our books. This mail includes letters both from contributors and readers. We thought we would share with you excerpts from some of the letters that really touched our hearts.

'I love all the books in the series I've read so far and am looking forward to the new ones coming out. It's a great feeling to know that animals in need are benefiting from these wonderful books.'

Mary, New Zealand

'Thank you for my copy of SMARTER than JACK; it is such a privilege to be able to contribute to animal welfare in this way. If I were asked what I would like to be remembered for in this life, there are only two things of great importance in my opinion: to know I have loved my family well enough, and to have helped relieve the suffering of animals as much as possible.'

Trish, Australia

'I must say thank you for my book, which arrived yesterday. I am delighted and enjoying it immensely. How glad I am that I found you!'

Joyce, England

'Thank you so very much for the wonderful SMARTER than JACK book! I enjoyed every word of it and will be purchasing some as gifts for family and friends. When I saw our dear old Jessie looking at me from the pages it was rather overwhelming, but I am so happy that many animal lovers will know of her now – what a gift to us.'

Sandy, Canada

'I first learned about SMARTER than JACK from a friend in New Zealand. The books are terrific – there are not enough books about animals and their special abilities and/or character out there.'

Sharman, Canadian writer living and working in South Korea

'The SMARTER than JACK stories always brighten my day and, although it doesn't surprise me that animals are so smart, it is a delight to read of the various ways in which they exhibit their smartness.'

Jenny, Australia

'I am writing not only to say thank you for my complimentary copy but also to congratulate you and all those who spent time in putting together such an enjoyable book. A great big "Well done". It is the sort of book one can leave on the coffee table to be picked up at leisure, when snippets can be read with pleasure from time to time.'

Phillip, England

'I just love the SMARTER than JACK book you sent us and think this is a great way to raise money and awareness for the SPCA.'

Hayley, New Zealand

'I have just read your new "Dogs are SMARTER than JACK". I am extremely impressed. The stories are wonderful. So many great dogs who continuously amaze us with their level of intelligence and problem solving. In each story I find similarities to the many special four-legged friends I have enjoyed over the years. I especially enjoyed all of the photos included in this issue. It provides added enjoyment to be able to see the fuzzy face, happy smile, or regal countenance of these real-life pets who have made such an impression on the people whose lives they have touched.

Keep up the good work. You are creating a history of the amazing intelligence that can be found in the animal kingdom and your books will be favourites for many years to come.'

Jill, Canada

Anthea, Lisa and Angie of SMARTER than JACK selecting stories

occurred. It had all taken place so quickly and miraculously that
seemed surreal.

often wonder how Tyson knew how to save Muskoka. I always
w he was a very special golden retriever, but on that February day
ecame an even more amazing dog. He became Muskoka's and
extraordinary hero.

oris Thompson
itchener, Ontario
anada

> Write to me ... ✉
>
> Doris Thompson
> 211 Daimler Drive
> Kitchener ON N2A 4C8
> Canada

legend of Paddy Tinley

own as 'clever dog' by the kids of Kalumburu in the Kimberley,
dy, our Border collie/Labrador, was much admired and made a
of. With us teaching at the school, he knew the last bell of the
meant he could come over and say hello. He also knew that the
nd of a motorbike meant a ride to the airport or fun and games
h the family.

On one such excursion with friends and their Jack Russell, Djindi,
nearby creek had swollen while we were swimming at a waterhole.
is caused some concern about getting back, as it was getting dark.
elected to have a go and ride the four-wheelers across anyway,
her than stay on the wrong side of the creek all night.

In the attempt, Djindi somehow got caught in the flooding waters
d got sucked down the creek, heading towards the main river.
ddy, realising the seriousness of the situation and worried about
s mate, raced down the riverbank ahead of Djindi. He jumped in

5

Heroic animals are lif

Our extraordinary hero

Every day my two golden retrievers, Tyson (
Muskoka (just three months old), would take m
the beautiful tranquil woods. In the thick of tl
pond, and in the frosty days of February the po
so I thought. Muskoka showed me otherwise.

As Muskoka set about exploring all the wo
in her puppy life, she encountered the ice. Sl
she slipped and slid on it in all directions. It w
watching a wee puppy trying to master the art
fun suddenly stopped when Muskoka fell into a

She tried to claw her way out of the cold dark w
I just stood there frozen. I didn't know what to do
get her I would break through the ice and then w
serious danger. We were too far into the forest to t
of sheer panic I called out to Tyson, 'Tyson, save
astonishment, he abandoned his rabbit hunting
the ice. He stuck his snout in the hole and cat
hind end through the air, sending her across the
safe ground.

The two dogs then carried on nonchalantly
happened. I still stood there frozen. I could not

the raging water and swam at an angle to meet the exhausted dog. He then moved close to her, caught her against his side and swam with her to the side of the bank. It left those of us watching stunned and tingling with goosebumps. He was lauded as a hero and given a special name tag by Djindi's owners, and is legendary in this part of the world.

Darrin and Leonie Tinley
Geraldton
Western Australia

Nick's special guardian

Nitro was the cutest little German shepherd pup I had ever seen. From the moment I saw him, back in 1998, I knew I wanted him.

My parents, who were missionaries, were always travelling and when I met Nitro we were residing in Monterrey, Mexico. I used to stare at him through the chain-link fence of our landlord's property and think how much I would love to have him. Our landlord said we could have him as he was the last in her litter of pups. She had planned on keeping him as a guard dog, but when she saw my little sister Natasha she thought she was so cute she gave the pup to her. Since I am the eldest in the family and was 14 years old at the time, Nitro became mine.

He had seemed so cute and perfect, but as soon as I picked Nitro up I realised there was a lot of things wrong with him as he was the boniest pup I had ever held. He was so furry you couldn't tell how malnourished and underweight he really was until you picked him up. His ears were infested with fleas and ticks and he had bloody diarrhoea.

69

After visits to the vet every two weeks for the next six months, he was still underweight, small and getting over coccidia, worms and many other parasites. Many people thought he wouldn't make it, others said we should put him down as he was never going to be a fully healthy dog. I wouldn't have it. I loved this dog and he was going to make it. And I was right: Nitro grew up to be a healthy, happy dog – the best dog we have ever had.

Nitro has always been my little brother Nick's guardian angel, as they are only a few months apart in age and so grew up together. When Nick was little he would sit on my father's shoulder, and Nitro would walk at heel beside my dad looking up at Nick, always keeping an eye on him. He has also saved Nick's life – not once, but twice.

One day when Nick was about one and a half years old, he managed to escape out of the house and into the yard on our big two acre property. We couldn't find him anywhere. Then we saw Nitro running towards the old well that was located out of sight in the front of the property behind our house.

The well had some old pieces of rotten wood placed on top of it, as it was an old well and not being used. Nick had started to climb up onto the well using the cement stones around it to elevate himself to the top. If he had got to the top and stood on the rotten wood he would surely have fallen to his death.

Nitro ran towards the well and jumped up on it. He was risking his life as the wood could have broken at any moment, but he was on top of the well without hesitation and barked straight into Nick's face. He barked and barked fiercely so that Nick wouldn't keep climbing. He stayed on top of the well barking until someone came running and scooped Nick up in their arms, away from the danger

Nitro always keeps a close eye on Nick

of the well. Thankfully, the wood didn't break and Nitro was fine
– however, he had risked his life for his little friend.

On another occasion we were in the process of building a fence
around the pool but it wasn't yet completed. Nick, being the runaway
child that he is, was off in an instant. Without anyone even noticing,
he went running towards the pool at full speed. That's when I saw
him – and pictured the worst.

Unfortunately, I was way across at the other end of the property.
I started to run towards him, but I knew I couldn't get to him in
time before he fell into the pool. Then I saw Nitro running straight
towards Nick. He went in front of him, barking at him from every

71

angle so that Nick had to stop running. He had stopped Nick from falling into the pool where he could have drowned, once again saving his life.

Today, both Nick and Nitro are lively seven-year-olds and Nitro is still always watching over Nick, as well as our newest addition, three-year-old Bonnie. We will always be indebted to him.

Shanti Vadnais
Winnipeg, Manitoba
Canada

Write to me …

email Shanti
shantivadnais@yahoo.com

Never say sheep are stupid!

We purchased the vacant block of land next to our property as a possible investment. To keep the grass short, we bought two sheep. They were so good that they soon ran out of grass to eat. So we fenced off part of our front lawn and allowed them to graze there. They were very quiet animals and no bother to us.

However, one day I became aware of a constant bleating outside. I went out on the deck and looked down onto the lawn. One of the sheep was standing there, looking up at the house and bleating. The other sheep was nowhere to be seen. As I watched, she would take a few steps towards the vacant section, turn and look at me and bleat. This action was repeated several times and it seemed that she wanted me to follow her, so I did. Eventually she led me right up the vacant section to the very furthest corner. Her companion had sunk into a sodden open ditch right up to her neck and was unable to get out.

I had to call on my neighbour and together we managed, with great difficulty, to pull the sheep out of the bog, watched anxiously by the heroine. It was clear to me that, having first got my attention and then being very persistent, she had saved her mate from certain death.

Mrs J Owler
Howick, Auckland
New Zealand

Little dog turns lifesaver

A little Yorkshire terrier was heading home. With her much loved 'mum' in the driver's seat, Tammie the terrier was tucked up in her usual spot. They were heading down a stretch of road which they'd travelled many times before – when all of a sudden something went horribly wrong.

The car veered off the road, rolled down a hill and slammed into trees, out of view of the road. As the traffic on the road above drove past none the wiser, Tammie sat in the back of the car scared, shocked, battered and bruised. Her owner was slumped unconscious and seriously injured in front.

Tammie knew something was wrong – very wrong – and she must have realised it was up to her to save her beloved mum.

This brave terrier set to work. She managed to free herself from the car wreck and, despite being in pain, made her way to the top of the hill. Showing no sign of fear, Tammie ran down the middle of the road – quite literally stopping traffic – until someone noticed the accident and called for help.

73

Paramedics were soon at the scene and rushed Tammie's mum to the hospital, while her heroic pooch was taken to the vet to recover from her traumatic ordeal.

Tammie made a full recovery, as did her loving owner, who may not have survived if it hadn't been for this brave act by her beloved little dog. Tammie isn't just a hero to her mum; she has also been recognised by the RSPCA, which awarded her the RSPCA WA Animal Valour Award.

Emma-Jane Morcombe
RSPCA
Western Australia

Eight lives left to live

Returning to Palmerston North after travelling around Australia for a few months, I felt the need to settle down and have a feline companion.

I decided to go to the local SPCA and 'just have a look'. Most of the cats there were older, and I really wanted a younger cat but not necessarily a kitten. I noticed this small bundle of grey and white fur huddled in the corner of its cage and asked the assistant about 'that one'. She advised me that he was six months old and it appeared he had been mistreated and dumped, which had made him into a little spitball. She told me, 'You won't want him, he's rather vicious.'

Disregarding her advice, I asked her to open the cage and let me have a look for myself. I talked away to him before reaching in to give him a pat, and he cowered away but let me stroke him. After stroking him for a couple of minutes, I picked him up, and he started to purr. Needless to say, the rest is history and I adopted Maverick.

Despite his ferocious beginnings, he must have made a good impression on Jazz, my flatmate's German shepherd, and the two of them would race around the house, chasing one another and having a grand old time.

Early one evening Maverick didn't come when he was called. After a couple of hours I was getting rather concerned as it certainly wasn't like him to miss a meal. As it grew dark I grew increasingly worried and paced the backyard calling for him. Then I heard this very plaintive meowing, which was coming from somewhere in the backyard. Looking around with the torch, I couldn't see him but could still hear him.

I raced back inside and grabbed Jazz, then took her outside and told her to find Maverick. She immediately went to the gate, behind which was an in-ground swimming pool. We opened the gate, shone the torch, and discovered Maverick swimming in a foot of water at the base of the pool. I leaped in the pool, scooped him up and took him inside. My poor wee white Maverick had turned green from the algae in the pool and was shivering from the cold. I ran a nice warm bath and gave him a shampoo and blow-dry, something nice to eat and a lot of hugs.

Maverick lived up to his name, having quite a few more scrapes and testing his remaining eight lives, but he gave me 13 years of love and companionship. To Jazz I will be eternally grateful.

Karen Feron
Plimmerton
New Zealand

My dog Satan was my angel

We had been held up for a few days at our beach weekender by a cyclone. Now the wind had passed, the sun was trying to break through and the ocean waves were in the process of calming down.

Having shared our small place with others needing shelter, it was quite a relief for all of us to get outside, and what better way to celebrate our 'release' than to go for a swim.

The sands of the beach had changed a little and I made my way through the still-pounding waves towards a sandbar that had formed not far from the water's edge.

Before I had time to explore the shape and size of the sandbar, there was a quite loud *huff* beside me and my dog Satan took a grip of my arm, firm enough to create big bruises. With more strength than I thought he possessed, he dragged me back out of the water.

It was some days later that some campers further along the beach, nearer the mouth of the creek, reported having recently seen a crocodile making its way upstream. If Satan hadn't forcibly removed me from the water, I may have ended up as that crocodile's next meal.

Florence Cooper
Cairns, Queensland
Australia

Believe it or not!

My 12-year-old granddaughter had a wee black mouse for a pet and her older sister had a pet cat called Jessie. One day while the mouse cage was being cleaned the little creature made a getaway through the open back door.

The whole family searched everywhere in their large garden and kept this up for a whole week. Then they gave up looking, much to my granddaughter's distress. She just adored her little pet.

Almost exactly two weeks later, Jessie – who always brings her trophy mice home for all to see and puts them in her bowl – came in the back door with a mouse in her mouth. Instead of her usual behaviour she went up to my daughter Pam, who was at the bench, but still didn't drop the mouse. Pam looked down and saw that it was a black mouse. She took it from the cat, only to find that there was not one bite or injury on it. Jessie had found my granddaughter's mouse and carried it home as gently as she would her own kittens.

This is hard to believe, I know, but it is perfectly true. Result – one happy child, and one very happy mouse now playing on his wheel.

Gwen Keene
Upper Hutt, Wellington
New Zealand

Valentine the wonder dog

Valentine is a beautiful mongrel who was donated to Hearing Dogs for Deaf People. She is now my hearing dog and has shown herself to be a paramedic, wonder dog and guardian angel.

Soon after I got Valentine, she alerted me to my father-in-law having fallen in the bedroom between the bed and the wall as he had had a stroke. I was out in the garden and had not heard anything, but Valentine realised something was wrong and, even though she had not been given a command, she ran to fetch me and took me back to where he was lying. He was later admitted to hospital.

© Hearing Dogs for Deaf People

June with Valentine

Valentine became quite ill, and was admitted to the veterinary hospital with viral enteritis and put on a drip. I was told that I had nearly lost her. Nevertheless she came through it, and after three days I brought her home. The vet told me not to work her, so I didn't.

One day it was raining. My husband went out to the garage while I was in the kitchen preparing the vegetables. Valentine started touching me, but I ignored her, saying, 'No, the vet said no titbits.' She went away and I turned back to the sink.

All of a sudden, Valentine came flying at my legs and I realised that she wanted me to follow her. She took me to the patio doors, where I found my husband collapsed on the patio in the pouring rain. My husband was admitted to hospital with a suspected brain haemorrhage.

Another time Valentine was a paramedic was when my grandson was about two and was playing out on the patio when a strong gust of wind blew him into a bush. Before my grandson started to cry – before we even realised what had happened – Valentine ran to him and started comforting him.

One day when we were out, Valentine again acted above and beyond her training. I was walking up the high street and went to cross a very busy road, stepping out between two parked lorries. I looked out and said to Valentine, 'It's all right, we can go.' Valentine would not cross, but kept backing towards the pavement. All of a sudden I looked up and there was a lorry passing at speed. I realised that I would have been underneath that lorry. Since then, Valentine will only let me cross on a pedestrian crossing.

Due to my hearing loss I lose my balance and fall over quite frequently. Recently, Valentine came to my aid when I got up in the early hours and it was still quite dark and I didn't put the light on. Coming back from the bathroom, I lost my balance and fell. Valentine came rushing out of the bedroom to see if I was all right. I had to tell her that I was okay before she would settle down in her sleeping position beside my bed.

Valentine is indeed a very heroic hearing dog, very kind and very loving to everyone she meets. To me, Valentine is not just my working dog but a very dear friend as well, and we work as one.

June J Beech
Wincanton, Somerset
England

'Nanny' Patches

My sons, our friends and our Jack Russell, Patches, used to go to the beach every summer, and we'd spend the day relaxing while the children played in the water or on the sand.

Patches was our children's 'nanny' and kept an eye on them by constantly rounding them up. Sometimes she would have to grab them by the hand or swimwear and pull them back to where we could see them. She would do this all day. When the children were playing in an area she deemed safe, she would come and sit by me and have a drink or a quick nap, always with her ears standing up. But the second she couldn't see or hear a child she would go on 'patrol' and round them up again.

One weekend – nearly 15 years ago now – we went to a popular beach that we hadn't been to before. After setting up the umbrellas and sunscreening all the children (the usual number was about ten), we told them not to go too far and prepared to relax. I told my sons (who, at about nine years old, were older than the others) to please stay together and keep an eye on the littlies – which was fine for half the day. Then they decided to go exploring in the sandhills, and so we took over the watching. My sons took Patches with them.

About an hour passed and I had just started out to look for them when Patches came running back to us, barking vigorously and looking behind her in the direction the boys had taken. I got up and followed her, as that is what she seemed to expect, and we went into the sandhills. Patches was still barking and running ahead, so I realised something was wrong and started to run too.

She led me to a gap between some sandhills where there was a creek that was very deep and dark. There were some people standing around the edges, pointing. I looked to where they were pointing and saw one of my sons floating face down in the water. The next thing I knew, Patches had dived into the creek and grabbed him by his swim shorts, but she couldn't quite pull him back to the edge. Then I realised there was a whirlpool motion in the water and Patches was getting caught in it too.

I dived in there after her, yelling to a couple of the others to get help, and swam quickly towards Patches. I grabbed her by the tail and tried to pull her back, while she hung onto my son. Then I felt a hand grab my leg and there was a man pulling me back too!

We made it back to the bank just as the ambulance people arrived. They performed CPR on my son and he survived. Our dearest pet Patches was given a big round of applause and treats from everyone who had watched the rescue – and heaps of cuddles from my son, who has never forgotten what she did to save his life.

Unfortunately, Patches has since passed away. Never has a dog been so precious to us as our best friend and 'nanny' Patches.

Karryn McKenna
Upper Hutt, Wellington
New Zealand

The smartest animal of all!

Many of our readers love to take photos of their pets reading (or sleeping) on SMARTER than JACK books – now, that is smart! We love getting these pictures and thought that they should no longer be kept hidden from public view. From now on, in each edition of SMARTER than JACK, we will publish the best new photo that we have received.

For submission information please go to page 146.

This photo of Jeff the cat is by Pat Reesby of Wellington, New Zealand. Pat receives a complimentary copy of this book.

Jeff agrees with the title of his book

6

Heroic animals make great friends

A feline defender

One balmy evening my husband and I were sitting on our front veranda with our shih-tzu Milo and cat Coco, when a couple stopped at the front of our house with two dogs, one of which was unleashed. Suddenly, the unleashed dog attacked Milo on our front lawn.

Out of nowhere sprang Coco, leaping onto the back of the dog. It stopped mauling Milo and turned on Coco, chasing her round the side of the house. The owners called their dog off and it returned to them.

Not realising what had happened, we had a few words with them and then went inside, only to find the house splattered with blood. The dog had ripped a five-inch wound in poor Coco's stomach which required hospitalisation.

Coco had saved her best friend Milo and was truly a brave cat. Her heroic actions were reported in the local paper.

June Green
Melbourne, Victoria
Australia

Write to me ...

email June
jgre3549@bigpond.net.au

Brave Coco stood up for Milo

Ginger's saviour

Scotty was a medium-sized dog of mixed lineage. He was our only dog for many years, then my sister got a cocker spaniel puppy we called Ginger. We lived on a farm a quarter of a mile from the highway, and we were always afraid someone would hit Ginger as he wasn't at all car-smart. He didn't seem to understand that he could be hurt or killed, so whenever we heard a car we'd run outside to find him.

When we were playing and making a fuss of Ginger, I'd look over at Scotty and he'd have such a sad look on his face. Having attention showered on the newcomer might have made him jealous but it didn't stop him from protecting Ginger when necessary. Scotty had a big and loving heart.

The first time I saw Scotty save Ginger's life, I couldn't believe my eyes. The car was coming round the house at a good speed, and I saw Scotty run in front of the car, putting himself between Ginger and the car tyres, and pull Ginger out of harm's way by his long ears. He saved Ginger's life many, many times by this ingenious method.

What a wonderful and brave dog he was to put himself in danger to save the little newcomer, who had stolen the limelight and some of the affection that previously had been his and his alone.

I don't think we'll ever have another dog as smart and brave as Scotty. He truly was a hero.

Sharon Anne Serbin
Regina, Saskatchewan
Canada

Write to me ... ✉
Sharon Anne Serbin
68 Carmichael Road
Regina SK S4R 0C5
Canada

Scampy's most heroic act

My hearing dog Scampy is a mongrel who has proven to be a lifesaver on a couple of occasions.

Once when Scampy and I were walking home from the supermarket, she suddenly pulled me and my trolley full of shopping over to some railings. As I looked up to see what the problem was, a taxi passed very close to both of us at frightening speed. Although I had not heard it coming, Scampy had realised the danger and acted on it.

However, Scampy's most remarkable heroic act involved my beloved elderly cat Simon. One evening Scampy and I had gone upstairs to bed. Simon came with us, then after a while wandered downstairs as he normally did. I was coming out of the bathroom to go to bed, when Scampy came out of the bedroom and alerted me. She then ran downstairs as if her life depended on it. Knowing that something was very wrong I followed her.

Scampy was staring at Simon as if not knowing what else to do, and then I saw that Simon had caught himself on a cord that was hanging on the banister. It had wound round his neck, and in trying to free himself he had wound it tighter and was beginning to choke to death.

How Scampy knew that Simon was in danger I shall never know, but she saved his life.

June Ironside
Eastbourne, Sussex
England

Write to me ... ✉

Mrs June Ironside
c/o Hearing Dogs for Deaf People
The Grange, Wycombe Road
Saunderton, Princes Risborough
Buckinghamshire
HP27 9NS
United Kingdom

Caring cows

Having always loved animals, it was no surprise – to anyone other than the landowner – that in no time at all I had such a rapport with the cattle that all I needed to do was say, 'C'mon girls, come get ya clean clothes on!' and they would all come up into the yard ready for dipping.

I helped many of the cows through birthing and I was often rescuing calves that had been caught up in wire, fallen into dams, or even got stuck in rusty old tins they had been investigating!

Scampy and June

The cattle were suffering badly after a fire had swept through and taken what little grass there was. We were all suffering from the drought conditions, and I would often bring them carloads of carrots and was constantly refilling troughs. This meant I was always there for them when they needed help.

Now, most people's perception of cattle seems to be that they are not very smart, but this is just so wrong! They live as a community, sharing the care of the young to the point of actually having a nursery tended to by one or two cows while the other mothers graze.

For me, the most amazing proof of how clever they are was when one of my favourites, Mama, was feeling poorly and our meanest cow, Diane, was sitting in a constant vigil over her.

I heard Diane bellowing and saw her heading towards the house in obvious distress. I went out to see what was wrong. Diane came up to the fence and kept looking back towards the dam, so I figured there must be a cow in the dam. As I came out the gate she ran ahead, then stopped to look back at me and bellowed with such urgency that I began to run.

As I neared where she stood, she looked away from the dam track towards the back of the yard, which made me think one of the calves was stuck in the bales again. However, as I turned to grab a rope she ran up to me and was making such a racket that I thought she was angry at me. I stepped out of reach behind the barn door (she was renowned for charging at you if she was upset with you for being near her calves).

From inside the barn I could see the other cattle grouped around something in the yard. As they saw me they all began to bellow in the way they do if there is trouble. Forgetting my own fear, I responded to theirs and ran towards them to see what was wrong.

As I got closer they all stood aside to reveal Mama lying flat on the ground. I knew straight away that there was definitely something wrong in the way she was lying, and felt my heart in my throat as I went over to see what it was.

Poor Mama was already dead and there was absolutely nothing I could do for her. As I knelt beside her, I shed a few tears. My heart was so full of love for these wonderful beasts that had such a strong sense of family that they too were mourning the loss of one of the matriarchs of their herd.

I was surrounded by them as they stood waiting expectantly for me to make it all right again. The trust they had in me was so strong, and it just gutted me to think they were so sure I could make this right.

As I turned to walk back to the house to phone the landowner, all I could do was say, 'Sorry darlin's but Mama is dead ... I can't fix this.' The slow mournful calls that rang out were gut-wrenching. I have never felt as bad as I did then, walking away without being able to fix it. They mourned her for two days and I spent as much time as I could talking to them and just sitting with them after her body had been removed.

Life is very hard for cattle in drought, as they truly mourn each loss of life.

Are cattle dumb beasts? You tell me!

Karen Trilford
Boonah, Queensland
Australia

Write to me ...

email Karen
wickedwildnwise@gmail.com

Cleo's gentle touch

Cleo is our nine-year-old golden Labrador, whose gentle nature continues to amaze me. She has a mother's nurturing approach to all living things she encounters, whether they be humans, dogs, cats – or even mice.

I take Cleo into the aviary every day when I feed the birds (mostly cockatiels). It does not bother the birds at all. In fact, sometimes they even land on her back.

One morning Cleo did not follow me into the aviary but stayed outside, intently looking at something in the wire. She had found a mouse who had got itself firmly stuck, with its head in one wire square and its body in the next square.

I went to pull it out, but decided it was stuck too firmly and that, if I pulled it, it could easily lose its head.

Cleo, however, was not convinced. She started gently pulling the mouse with the tips of her front teeth. Whenever the resistance was too strong she stopped and got another hold, and she continued like this until she had pulled the mouse free. She placed the mouse on the lawn, nudged it with her nose and watched it run into the garden. Then she trotted to the aviary door and waited to be let in.

I would not have believed this unless I had seen it. To see an animal as big and strong as Cleo – who can easily crush a large bone with one chomp – then use the same mouth to gently rescue a little mouse was heart-warming.

I believe people can learn a lot from animals – like Cleo – who approach life with a refreshing blend of no fear and no aggression.

Dedicated to Peppie, who gave me my love for dogs.

Peter Bishenden
Toormina, New South Wales
Australia

Sylvie's unexpected act of kindness

I was outside gardening one day with my three dogs: Minny, a Pomeranian cross, Delilah, an Australian terrier, and Sylvie, a Jack Russell. Being blind, Delilah walks quite cautiously around the home, and it was no surprise when she walked slowly round the yard before deciding to walk up towards the house.

As she headed towards the veranda doorway it looked as if she was going to collide with the door frame. Before I could say anything, Sylvie whizzed up and placed herself between the wooden door frame and Delilah, providing something soft for Delilah to bump into. She stayed there until Delilah had passed safely through the doorway. I stood there amazed at this unexpected act of kindness and gave Sylvie a yummy treat soon after!

Simone Dillon
Watsonia, Victoria
Australia

The lion shall lie down with the lamb

Pit bulls have a terrible reputation. However, I recently saw something which goes a long way to persuade me that some aren't quite as black as they are painted.

Friends of mine have two of the breed, an old male and a young female. Both are neutered and much loved. The dogs have their own kennels, and also share a three acre paddock with a number of ewes who, at this time of the year, are either about to lamb or have done so and are trailing new lambs in their wake.

I was watching the dogs from the lounge window as they napped in the shelter of the long hedge. As I studied them a ewe arrived with two very small lambs, both babies clearly feeling the chilly wind.

91

The ewe marched over to the dogs and stamped her front foot. The dogs looked up and she stamped again – a demanding, authoritative stamp. Obediently both dogs rose and moved a couple of metres along the hedge, leaving the better shelter and nicely warmed spot for the two tiny shivering lambs to collapse onto. As they lay down the female dog returned, checked them over with an expression of concern and then, reassured, went back to join her companion.

I was left smiling and wondering if this was the New Zealand version of 'and the lion shall lie down with the lamb'.

Lyn McConchie
Norsewood
New Zealand

Brotherly devotion

It was a late summer day. With nothing urgent pending, I thought I would go down to the lower paddock and check out the last of the season's wild blackberries.

I duly set off with my containers, protective clothing and a wasp deterrent. I'm never without at least one of my cats to share my outdoor activities, so I called out to them, 'Who's coming walkies?' My ten-month-old ginger cat Bruno was the first to prick up his ears and come bounding after me, followed by his tortoiseshell sister Bree. No sight or sound of the other six cats.

I set off for the lower paddock, with Bree and Bruno pacing on either side of me. Bruno was in a playful mood and would take off every so often in a mad dash through the grass, with only his bushy tail visible. He would flip through and over the long grass, then return to us. This continued until we got to our destination.

Playful Bruno

Bruno and I went down to the blackberry patch, while Bree remained behind in the lower paddock. Bruno and I were having an enjoyable time. He was pouncing on my hands as I picked the berries and playing his own little games of 'catch the berry'.

Meanwhile, Bree had started mewing to us from the lower paddock, quietly at first and then more urgently. Bruno seemed concerned and kept looking in Bree's direction as her mewing got louder and louder. He took off towards her, stopped, looked back at me, ran towards me, stopped again, then looked back at Bree as if he couldn't make up his mind. Finally, he must have decided that Bree really needed him and bounded over to her to see if she was okay.

They met up under the pine trees, rubbing noses and sniffing each other. Was Bree communicating to Bruno that she didn't want to be left by herself in the lower paddock? Perhaps she was, because they then walked calmly up the track back to the home paddock side by side, just like a couple of human friends. It was rather cute to observe Bruno's display of brotherly devotion. He had been having fun down at the berry patch, but seemed to consider Bree's happiness more important than his own.

I finished my picking and headed back, not expecting to see Bruno and Bree until dinnertime – but there they were, sitting side by side under the pine trees in the middle paddock. It seemed like they had been waiting for me, because as soon as I appeared they got up and came to meet me and both gave me a smooch or two. And so we finished our walk as we had started out – with me in the middle and one cat on either side.

It gives you the 'warm fuzzies' when animals accept you as one of them.

June Spragg
Warkworth
New Zealand

Write to me ... ✉
June Spragg
453 Westcoast Road
Ahuroa RD 1
Warkworth 1241
New Zealand

Keeping it in the family

My daughter Barbara has always been an animal lover and dedicated to rescuing homeless and unfortunate animals and birds. When her pedigree Irish setter produced a litter of pups, she kept them all in case they were not properly looked after. They are now two years old and very well behaved.

One day recently, Barbara heard a single woof. On investigation, she found all seven setters (mother and offspring) sitting in a close circle on the lawn. In the middle of the circle was a little bird which the cat had caught. The dogs were guarding it and keeping the cat away until Barbara could come out and rescue it. After an hour in a special cage with a hot-water bottle, the bird had recovered and was able to fly away.

Another day, Barbara saw a cat boxing a dog's nose. She took the dog's face in her hands to comfort him and saw a foot and a tail hanging out of his mouth! She squealed, the dog opened his mouth, and a little mouse hopped out and ran away, completely unhurt.

It seems as if these dogs have inherited the family's need to rescue unfortunate animals.

Jean Collins
Tauranga
New Zealand

Our little lifesaver

We first met Trojan, a three-month-old black miniature poodle, when he chose us ahead of the little girl we had planned on picking up. He certainly lived up to his name – a right little Trojan. We loved him instantly, and by the time we discovered his epilepsy there was no way he was going back to the breeder.

He loved the days when the kids were swimming in the pool. He would end up waterlogged, as he often missed the corners and went in for a dip, then swam confidently to the steps to get out and race round and round again. He had the knack of jumping onto the floating beanbed and swanning across the water like a ship's captain.

My parents also owned a miniature poodle, Tolley, who was a shy, quiet little girl. She became blind as she aged. We were babysitting her one night and at about 2 am we heard Trojan barking and barking. I called to him to come inside and be quiet. No luck – he just kept barking in a very agitated way. I called Tolley and reached out of bed

95

Little Trojan the lifesaver

to see if she was nearby. She wasn't there, which was unusual as she normally kept close to me.

I felt disturbed and a little sickened. I raced out to the pool and called Troj but he still wouldn't come. I turned on the lights and there he was, leaning out over the water near the filter box. Tolley was hanging on by her claws from the filter box ledge, her nose barely out of the water. She must have been there for ages, as the pads on her back feet were bleeding from trying to get out.

The story has a happy ending, as – after a trip to the vet, treatment for submersion and the pads on her feet bandaged – Tolley was fine. Trojan earned his lifesaving award that night.

Jenni Mulholland
Mt Helena
Western Australia

Write to me ... ✉
email Jenni
mojen@bigpond.net.au

7

Heroic animals prevent tragedies

Bertie knew something was wrong

My Yorkshire terrier Bertie may be one of the smallest working hearing dogs, but he has more than made up for his lack of stature by being indispensable not only to me but also to others he meets along the way.

Bertie's worth has never been in any doubt, but recently he acted above and beyond the call of duty when he visited me during my stay in hospital. He was curled up asleep at my feet when he suddenly sat bolt upright and became extremely agitated. I tried to calm him down, but he kept staring at the lady dozing in the next bed and made it very clear to me that there was something very wrong.

Eventually the nurse came over to see what all the commotion was, and on checking the lady immediately called the resuscitation team. The lady's oxygen level had dropped so much that she had stopped breathing, but everyone except Bertie had assumed she was asleep. The hospital staff were amazed and made a huge fuss of Bertie, as his actions had helped save her life.

Gill Stevenson
Ceredigion
Wales

Bertie and Gill

Sonny the rat sniffs out big trouble

One night, I was lying in bed petting my rat Sonny – a runt Siamese with a handsome chocolate point nose and bum, a silky lustrous beige coat and scarlet eyes.

Even though there's a travel cage with a water bottle on it in my bedroom, I always put Sonny and his friends back into the 'rat room' before I go to bed. On this particular night, I grew so sleepy that I thought, 'To heck with it' and I leaned over and put him on the floor for the night. My king-size bed is also extra-high, so I thought there would be no way Sonny could climb up and disturb me while I slept.

I don't live by myself, but on this night I was alone in the house except for Sonny and his gang. I awoke to him chattering as he tickled my ear with his long whiskers.

Exasperated, I took out my earplugs. 'Aw, Sonny! You're a pesky little pest! Let me sleep.' I grabbed him, reached down and plunked him on the floor. As I drifted off, earplugs in hand, I heard a determined *scritch scratch* as Sonny made the colossal climb up my 'Mount Everest' bed. He scampered over and squeaked in my ear.

Contrary to the popular notion that rats squeak, I've found that it's a sound they rarely make. The only time, in fact, that I've ever heard this sound was when I accidentally stepped on a tail.

As I remembered this I bolted awake. I wondered if Sonny was injured. In a bold squirrel-like move he descended the quilt, made a long jump and – *plop!* – hit the floor. He ran to the door, squeaking loudly. I had never seen behaviour like this. I was puzzled. Was he lonely for his chums and having some sort of panic attack?

I opened the door. Sonny surprised me by racing past the 'rat room' and on down the hall. I followed. Before I reached the kitchen, I smelled the smoke. A pot – in which all the water had evaporated

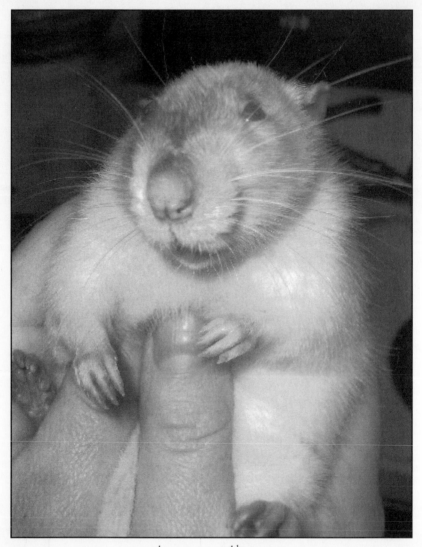

Clever Sonny used his nose

– was burning on the stove, the element was glowing red and the smoke was getting thicker. (Fixing the smoke alarms had been on my 'to do' list.)

I nearly stepped on poor Sonny, who stood behind me, his whiskers twitching frantically.

I put the pot in the sink and ran cold water over it, turned on the fan and opened the back door to let the air in. I remembered that I had put the water on to make tea (we had recently moved in and the electric kettle was still packed).

I scooped up my valiant rat, held his cute face in front of mine and said aloud, 'Without your help, the house could have burned down. I am so sorry I called you a pesky little pest. You are *not* pesky – and you're certainly not a pest. You are a bright and brave rat, Sonny. What you *are* is a hero.'

Sheila Morrison
Gabriola Island, British Columbia
Canada

Write to me ... ✉

Sheila Morrison
986 Lewis Close
Gabriola Island BC V0R 1X2
Canada
or email Sheila
smorrisonhamilton@yahoo.ca

Insightful Stumpy to the rescue

My father grew up on an island near the entrance to Gippsland Lakes in Victoria, and his family had a Border collie/Labrador cross named Stumpy. He did some remarkable things.

One morning at breakfast, Grandpa heard a scream and the sound of a dogfight, so he picked up his rifle and raced out to the backyard. At a glance he could see what had happened.

A kelpie/dingo cross had attacked my Uncle Norman – a toddler at the time – and bitten his head. Stumpy had come to the rescue and got the dingo by the throat. Grandpa shouted and the dingo dropped Norman and ran up a leaning tree. Grandpa killed him with his first shot.

Another day my Aunt Nina was returning from Lakes Entrance (the town) in a flat-bottomed boat when she capsized. She had a pound of butter in one hand and a string of sausages around her neck, and she clung to the bottom of the boat with her free hand. Grandma and the older girls could see her predicament, as the strong tide was carrying her relentlessly towards the entrance. They were desperate as they had no means to rescue her but prayer.

Grandpa and the boys were swimming cattle (moving them across the water) at Duck Point about six miles away. Stumpy became agitated and ran to the boat and then back to the men, pulling at their clothes. They got the message and rowed as fast as they could, with Stumpy – very pleased – standing in the bow. Once they rounded the point they could see what had happened, so they rowed even faster, reaching Nina just where the waves were beginning to break, and she was saved.

How did Stumpy – with Nina well out of his sound and sight – know?

Dr L H McMahon
Wahroonga, New South Wales
Australia

Bentley used his initiative

My hearing dog Bentley, a Norfolk terrier cross, is quite simply a lifesaver and has acted heroically on more than one occasion.

A few years ago Bentley saved the life of my other dog, Poacher. Poacher and Bentley were out in the garden and I was inside. Suddenly Bentley raced inside, found me and then alerted me by touching me. He led me out into the garden, where I found poor Poacher choking. I rushed her to the vet, where it was discovered that a piece of food had got stuck in her throat.

Bentley's lifesaving actions do not apply only to dogs. I suffer from vertigo, and a couple of years ago I collapsed while in the garden. Bentley immediately ran into the house to find my wife Barbara, alerted her and then took her to where I was lying. Bentley's prompt actions prevented a more serious outcome.

However, it is Bentley's more recent heroic acts that quite literally saved my life. In June 2004 I had a minor stroke and, for the several months before I had a pacemaker fitted, my heart would stop at irregular intervals during the night. As a result of this, Barbara had to be constantly aware when I stopped breathing so she could give me a push to make me start again.

Although Barbara tried her best to stay awake to ensure she could keep nudging me, one night she fell asleep. She was woken by Bentley, who went round to her side of the bed and touched her to wake her up. She was then able to push me to get my heart started again.

Another time I had a particularly bad night. After the ambulance crew had gone and I had settled to sleep, Barbara knew she would not sleep again so at 5 am she went to sit in the lounge. Half an hour later Bentley came into the lounge, touched her and led her back to the bedroom, where again I had stopped breathing.

Colin and Bentley

This is all the more remarkable since Bentley has been trained predominantly to alert me – not Barbara – to sounds. The fact that he used his training and initiative to realise something was wrong and to tell Barbara is amazing.

Since I had my pacemaker fitted, all three of us now get a good night's sleep!

Colin James
Bournemouth, Dorset
England

Tibby knew before we did

Many years ago, when I was a high school girl in England, my family had a pet cat who had recently become the mother of five kittens. The weather was wet and cold and Tibby kept her kittens in a box on the hearth, next to the fire.

One morning my mum came out of the kitchen and, to her amazement, Tibby had jumped onto the dining room table and was feeding her babies there. Mum scolded her and returned her to the box near the fire. A while later Mum noticed that Tibby and her kittens had disappeared. She searched and found them on the landing at the top of the stairs. Puzzled, she left them there.

Later on that day, cars with loudspeakers drove through the streets, warning us that the river had broken its banks – which had never happened before.

From our school high up over the valley, we watched in awe as the waters turned the suburbs into a lake and flooded the houses to a depth of five feet.

105

Unable to get home until the following day, wading through mud and sludge, we all heard the strange tale of Tibby and her kittens.

'She knew,' Mum said. 'She knew before anyone that the house was going to be flooded, and all she wanted to do was save her family.'

Edith Mazzone
Sydney, New South Wales
Australia

Jaz showed us that we'd made the right choice

For the first 18 months of life with our young Jack Russell terrier Jaz, I seriously doubted our choice of puppy as I struggled to train him and contain his wilful and determined nature. Often he tested me to the limit, and I would be left floundering and cursing in his wake as he took off down the road on yet another joyful excursion. One frightening winter night, however, he justified our choice in an unbelievable way.

Every night his soft warm bed is placed in our bedroom and we cover our duvet with a sheet. Every night, of course, Jaz chooses to sleep on top of the sheet and, if he can get away with it, wedges himself between the two of us, emitting noisy indignant moans if we dare to move.

This particular night my husband was away and I was sleeping the deep sleep of the exhausted, with Jaz in his usual place beside me. In my dreams I heard a dog constantly whining. This noisy dream went on and on and eventually woke me, whereupon I realised that it wasn't a dream. Jaz was standing on the floor right beside me, and my electric blanket was on fire, smoke curling up in a spiral right beside where I had been sleeping. Although he had an escape route himself Jaz didn't leave my side, and if it wasn't for his persistent whining I doubt whether I would have woken up in time.

Jaz – man's best friend!

Cheryll Gadsby
Hawera
New Zealand

Write to me ... ✉
Cheryll Gadsby
5 Quin Crescent
Hawera
New Zealand

Boisterous Jaz alerted Cheryll just in time

Dodger – my hero

I have been severely deaf since childhood. Before I got my spaniel cross Dodger from Hearing Dogs for Deaf People, I felt isolated and was concerned about being unaware if there was a fire or a burglary in my home.

Most days Dodger and I walk to town from our house. It is a distance of two miles and takes about half an hour.

On one occasion last September we were nearing the town centre and were waiting at a set of traffic lights to go across the road. All the lights must be red before one can cross.

We were waiting for the 'green man' light on the pedestrian crossing to appear and the appropriate noise to sound, but when they did Dodger didn't move. I looked down at him. His head was back and there was no way he was going to go. I said, 'What's up, Dodger?' and bent down slightly to speak to him.

The next moment, although the lights were still red, a cyclist came whizzing round the corner really, really fast! If I had forced Dodger to move there no doubt would have been a collision and I don't know what injuries I would have sustained. (In 2001 a man was killed by a cyclist on a pavement in town.)

Thanks to Dodger all was well that ended well, and we crossed the road safely. I don't know how he knew the bicycle was coming round the corner but he did.

Alison Chester
Merseyside
England

Write to me ...   ✉

Alison Chester
c/o Hearing Dogs for Deaf People
The Grange, Wycombe Road
Saunderton, Princes Risborough
Buckinghamshire
HP27 9NS
United Kingdom

Sebastian to the rescue

Living in the middle of a cornfield, I was always concerned for my little white cat Happy as, when she was curled up in the grass, I was sure she must look like a rabbit to the eagles and hawks that regularly circled overhead.

Out in the yard one day, I heard Happy hiss in alarm and turned to see a hawk swooping down on her. I ran towards her, but my German spitz Sebastian got there first and scared the hawk off. He stayed with her until I reached them and, thanks to Sebastian, Happy was unhurt.

Leanne Westerling
Laidley, Queensland
Australia

Heroic Sebastian

The cat knew what to do

Recently, a young teenage girl in my home town was woken by her cat standing on her chest licking her face. She then realised that she could smell smoke, and raced to wake her parents, brother and sister.

They were lucky enough to all get out of the house (with the cat, of course) before the entire tiled roof caved in. The fire had apparently started in the ceiling.

Without the cat the family would no doubt have perished, as the house was gutted in minutes.

Ivodell Hyde
Murray Bridge
South Australia

Please help my mom!

Robbie is my ten-year-old Highland terrier. I had wanted a Westie, but all the breeders had year-long waiting periods. I found Robbie when I went into a pet store to buy some cat food. He was very ill and they had put him on sale. The minute we locked eyes I knew he had to be mine. It took me three months to nurse him back to health. He still has some very odd quirks due to his younger days, but you could not ask for a more loyal friend.

About a year after I got him, I had extensive facial surgery and was sent home the same day. My friend from out of town came to stay and look after me. Of course, Robbie never left my side. It was difficult even to get him off my bed so that I could go to the bathroom!

The day after my operation I woke up and decided I could no longer stand the dried blood that was all over my bandages and in my hair. In my drug-induced stupor I decided to have a shower. Everyone else in the house was sleeping. While I was turning on the water and stumbling round the bathroom getting ready, Robbie took it upon himself to get help. He ran into the room where my friend was sleeping and started removing the blankets from her, corner by corner.

Once he had her totally uncovered, he started pushing at her back with his little black nose. When she finally woke up, he made direct eye contact with her and then beetled off back to my bathroom. My friend got the message and came rushing after him. Needless to say, I was rescued and put safely back to bed.

Robbie is now a living legend in both our houses. When you look at him you wouldn't think he has so much intelligence, but I know better. He has repaid me over and over again for rescuing him those many years ago. Robbie is my true friend and hero.

Sue Turgoose
Surrey, British Columbia
Canada

Megan's innovative thinking saved the day

My husband Trevor's hearing dog Megan is a terrier-type mongrel selected by Hearing Dogs for Deaf People from a rescue kennel. Trevor's life has totally changed since Megan arrived – and one day she also saved his life.

The day started as did any market day. We went first to Shopmobility to pick up Trevor's scooter. As usual, Megan sat on the scooter by his feet. Then we went our separate ways.

I was doing some shopping when I heard an ambulance siren. Not thinking, I downed tools and ran to where I thought Trevor might

111

be to make sure he was out of the way, but a stallholder stopped me and told me not to worry. He said that the little dog had touched Trevor's leg, then jumped off the scooter and lain down in the danger position. Trevor looked round, saw the ambulance and pulled over to let it pass.

What is so amazing is that Megan had never been trained for this specific situation, but she quickly put together what she knew and came up with her own solution. The stallholder and ambulance men said, 'What a wonderful dog you have.'

Trevor had left school at 16 and gone out to work. After 37 years of service he had to take early retirement because of ill health, and had almost given up on life. Then Trevor started taking Megan out and meeting new people, and slowly his confidence started to come back. After six months they were asked to represent the deaf in West Suffolk for the Queen's Jubilee at their cathedral. Trevor started work at a workshop for the disabled, and Megan goes with him.

They are now seen around our town and Trevor has been asked to sit on the local residents' association as a disability adviser. They have both achieved so much in only one year of working together. Megan has done so much to help Trevor overcome problems in his difficult and traumatic life.

Jean Larke
Bury St Edmunds, Suffolk
England

Write to us … ✉

Jean and Trevor Larke
34 Gloucester Road
Bury St Edmonds, Suffolk
IP32 6DN
United Kingdom

8

Heroic animals provide protection

Whiskers to the rescue

Our old sheepdog Whiskers had been with us since he was a pup. He and my husband were inseparable.

Whiskers was terrified of thunder, and we knew by his actions – well before any weather forecaster told us – when a storm was on the way. He would hide, shivering and frightened, as far back as he could get under anything in the shed. He dug great burrows under machinery, workbenches – anywhere to hide away.

One day, Whiskers had been cowering in any dark corner he could find so we knew a storm was coming. That night my husband was a couple of miles away from the house, finishing seeding for the day, when the storm struck violently. Lightning was forking dangerously and thunder was crashing. Suddenly, as my husband ran through the driving rain to the truck, Whiskers appeared out of the dark.

In spite of his terror, Whiskers had braved a two mile run through the storm to get my husband and bring him home.

Doreen Simpson
Milang
South Australia

Security bird

I never thought birds could be so clever and affectionate until we bought Pina, a cinnamon-coloured cockatiel. Pina's antics took us all by surprise, but none more so than on the day he decided to play a security guard.

Every night before we went to sleep, I would turn on the security alarm and it would beep twice. In the morning the alarm beeped three times to signal that it had been turned off. Pina soon caught on to this pattern and would beep twice when he was put to bed. At 6 am the characteristic three beeps could be heard coming from his cage, letting us know that he'd woken up and was 'turning off' the alarm.

One day I was at home alone when two of my brother's friends came looking for him. Pina had been in the front bedroom and had seen these 'strangers' walk past. Before I could answer the door I heard two beeps coming from the bedroom. Pina was letting me know that the alarm had been 'turned on' and to be on alert. After I'd turned my brother's friends away I walked into the front bedroom to check on Pina – just in time to hear his three beeps giving me the 'all clear'.

Adareeka Jayasinghe
Sinnamon Park, Queensland
Australia

We'll never forget Susie

It was 1947 in Pakistan. My sister, my two brothers and I played in the dry, dusty yard that was our back garden. With us were our two small spaniel cross dogs Susie and her puppy Scally (short for scallywag, he was well named). They were our best friends and went everywhere with us.

The heat was oppressive and my mother came out to see if we wanted a drink. She looked across the yard and, looking terrified, put her hand to her mouth and hissed loudly, 'Children, get in, mad dog!' A rabid pariah dog had entered the yard. The poor thing was foaming at the mouth. My brothers shot up a tree and stayed there out of reach, but the sick dog was between me and my sister and safety.

Snarling, the dog crept towards us. Susie could take no more! She went for the dog and there was a vicious fight that seemed to go on forever. Susie ended up victorious but badly bitten.

We had to keep away from Susie as we knew rabies was fatal. We gathered up Scally and went indoors. It was a dreadful day. The next day, after Susie had been buried under the tree, we took her puppy with us and sadly laid flowers on her grave. We vowed we would never forget our valiant little dog, and we never have.

We are all in our sixties now but we often talk about the day that 'Susie saved our lives'!

Bridget Egan
Broadstairs, Kent
England

Write to me …
email Bridget
egans@bushinternet.com

Buster wasn't laughing

Back in the 1930s my family lived on a farm in Saskatchewan.

It was a February day – my birthday. A neighbourhood girl came over to play and suggested we ride on the sleigh. A winter storm had left a big bank of snow in our yard, just right for a nice ride from the top down to near the corner of the porch. Our dog Buster enjoyed each run as he ran down beside us, bouncing along happily.

Then my friend suggested that, instead of the two of us sitting on the sleigh, I should go down alone and lie on my stomach. It was a trick as she was actually going to administer a few 'birthday whacks' to my bottom, but I hadn't caught on to her plan.

Off I started and she raised her hand for the first birthday whack. She soon stopped when Buster grabbed her arm. Our family pet was not going to let my friend hit me! He left no marks on her arm, but that day I saw a protective side to our dog that I hadn't seen before.

Marion Underwood
Regina, Saskatchewan
Canada

Write to me ... ✉
Marion Underwood
6-635 McRead Place
Regina SK S4T 7R3
Canada

My watch birds

I have two birds, a pink and grey galah and a grey weiro. They are both nine years old. I call them my watch birds because they look after me. I am 84 years old and they hear more than I do. They seem to know this and try to help me.

The weiro hears the postman's bike when he is streets away and lets me know he is coming. Alerted solely by her squeaking, I go to the letterbox 30 metres away and there is something in it for me. She also squawks when she hears the engines of my friends' cars to let me know they are coming.

They always squawk if anyone comes near my house or through my gate. The weiro knows the sound of my visitors' footsteps and tells me when they are still 30 or 40 metres away, around the corner and out of sight. Her ears are definitely better than mine!

One time when my doctor visited me at my home, he led me into my bedroom to examine me. My weiro went berserk, screaming as loud as she could. I knew I was not in any danger, but I am sure she was trying to protect me. She kept her eyes on him until he left the house.

Both birds really look after me. They don't like me going out, but when I come in the gate they start calling to me as they are so glad I've come home (I think they sleep while I am out).

We all nap together in the same room but, if I move even slightly, the galah's pink head pops up quickly before I can get up. They are great company for me.

Mrs K Marshall
Hillarys
Western Australia

Write to me … ✉

Mrs K Marshall
c/o Smarter than Jack
PO Box 27003
Wellington
New Zealand

Our champion

The bark of our young kelpie bitch Doreen woke me from my sunny springtime stupor. It was followed by squeals of laughter from my two daughters, Angie (eight) and Lara (five). They were walking down the path to play at the edge of our dam.

'Doreen's acting funny, Dad,' they called. When I arrived to investigate, I saw Doreen circling the girls and pushing them back up the path with her chocolate brown body. She then ran over to a small clump of bush and circled around it, barking furiously.

I told the girls to stay where they were while I went to see what she was barking at. Inside the bush was a rather large red-bellied black snake, just out of hibernation. Although these snakes are timid, they will attack if disturbed – and my girls would have disturbed this one if Doreen hadn't stopped them.

Brave Doreen – who had been born the previous winter and so had never seen a snake before – had somehow sensed the danger the girls were in and tried to warn them.

Doreen, our chocolate brown champion!

Jim Howe
Kiama, New South Wales
Australia

Write to me ...

email Jim
jimandjanet@fishinternet.com.au

Tyson could act tough when he needed to

I adopted Tyson from my local RSPCA centre when he was four years old. He was a mixture of Dobermann, German shepherd and Staffordshire bull terrier and had been at the centre for a long time because he looked rather vicious.

In reality he was the sweetest-natured dog – a bit of a coward if the truth be known. He would cower away from anyone who raised their voice near him and he was always a bit wary of men. However,

Tyson proved he wasn't really a DOPErmann

he was a very placid and laid-back dog and he never ever barked. In fact, he was such a dope that if anyone ever asked me what breed he was I'd say, 'He's a DOPErmann!'

One night I saw a very different side of him. I was alone upstairs in my house when I heard the sound of someone trying to break in through the back door. To say I was scared would be an understatement, but I knew I had to do something as I couldn't just let my home be violated. Without really thinking I rushed down the stairs and hurtled into the kitchen, to see the silhouettes of three or four men trying to break down the back door.

My instincts told me my dog would protect me. Heaven only knows why – remember that Tyson never barked and was wary of men. Nevertheless, I opened my mouth and the words – clearly directed at Tyson – 'See them off!' came out. He was out of his bed like a rocket. He ran to the back door, curled back his lips displaying his impressive fangs and barked like mad. It was as if he'd been a professional guard dog all his life. Needless to say, faced with such an apparently vicious adversary, the would-be burglars took one look at him and fled.

With shaking hands I managed to unlock the back door and let Tyson out, and he ran out and continued barking until the men had well and truly gone. When he was satisfied that all was well he came back up the path, wagging his tail and looking up at his biscuit tin for a treat.

I could hardly believe the way he'd behaved that night, it was so out of character. The instant it was over he reverted to the soppy old softy I knew and loved.

During the 12 years of his life with me I only ever heard him bark on one other occasion.

Tyson loved people – even the vet – and everyone who met him loved him back. He died a few years ago, aged 16, and is buried in my garden so he'll always be near me – my friend and protector.

Eileen Hayes
Cheltenham, Gloucestershire
England

One of Smokey's nine lives

When I was growing up my family had a cat called Smokey. She lived to be 16 and it would be fair to say she used up every one of her nine lives before she left this world. If there was trouble to be found, Smokey would find it!

She used one of her lives protecting my brother and me one summer afternoon. We were in our backyard bouncing away quite happily on our trampoline when I noticed Smokey bashing her head against the fence. We stopped bouncing and watched her for a moment. She looked as if she was dancing, jumping around on the paving stones and twisting this way and that. We got off the trampoline and walked towards her. She started hissing at us and it was then that my brother yelled 'Snake!' and ran off to get our mum, who was talking to our neighbour.

Mum came over, convinced it was just a 'legless lizard' until she saw just what it was Smokey had bailed up against the fence. Our 'legless lizard' was in fact a two metre long dugite! Dugites are dangerously venomous snakes. Smokey must have discovered it and had cornered it to prevent it from coming into the garden. It was wrapped around her middle and she had her paws around its head.

121

Mum ordered us inside while the neighbour ran home to get help. The neighbour seemed to take forever to come back, and suddenly the snake had disentangled itself from Smokey and was making its way towards Mum. She grabbed a shovel that was close by and had it raised above her head, preparing to hit the snake, when our other neighbour appeared out of nowhere with a rake. He pushed Mum out of the way and disposed of the snake in a very efficient manner.

Once all the commotion had died down we discovered that Smokey was nowhere to be seen. My brother said he had seen her jump over the fence when the snake turned towards Mum. We went looking for her and found her curled up in the nearby bush. Poor Smokey had been bitten by the snake and was not in a good way. We rushed her to the vet, who said there wasn't a lot we could do but wait and see. She was a sick old puss for a few days, but made a full recovery and was as good as new in no time.

After that incident Smokey carried a bit more weight – I think it had something to do with the extra milk and treats she got for being our hero.

Justine Brothers
Wickham
Western Australia

Bandette gave me something to live for

Bandette was a husky cross puppy. I didn't choose her, she chose me, but I loved her. She was my hero. I read a quote once that said something about 'becoming the person my dog thinks I am' and for me that is very true – she thought I was wonderful.

Bandette with friends Chuck and Sandi

I had a very turbulent and abusive childhood and I had tried to end my life a number of times by the age of 13. That is when Bandette came along. She was so smart and loyal and cute. She learned to open doors at six months old and would sneak into my room just to be with me; that was her greatest joy. She beat me to school every morning and waited there for me too.

One night I was babysitting about a block away from our house. It was late and dark when I started walking home. A yellow sports car started following me and I began to get very nervous. I was about two houses away from home, but it seemed like a mile when the car stopped and a man started to get out. I could hear my two dogs barking in our house. So I did the only thing I could think of – I screamed. Bandette and my other dog, Musko, jumped out of a second-storey window and raced to my side, arriving there in a matter of seconds. Bandette stayed right next to me with her body

123

between me and that car, while Musko chased the man back into his car and down the street. When it was all over I found that both dogs had been injured when they jumped – Bandette hurt her leg and Musko broke the end of his tail.

Many times Bandette put herself between me and danger, and she made me believe I was worth loving. She saved my life that night, I am sure of it – and for 13 years she gave me something to live for. She tolerated children, cats and all sorts of awful things just to be around me.

When she died I had her cremated so she could always be with me. Since being with me was the only thing she ever wanted, how could I say no?

Patricia M Kroeker
Waldheim, Saskatchewan
Canada

Beware of the kookaburra

Oscar was a kookaburra (a bird native to Australia) we hand-reared on raw meat. He was a little ball of fluff with a big beak who later became our chief rat catcher and snake tamer.

Oscar loved to be noticed, and as he got older he developed (prompted by me) a full-throated laugh to put the kookaburra that feautured on the opening sequence of the Cinesound newsreel films to shame.

He was an everyday kookaburra with a kink. I sometimes think he really believed he was a bantam. He was fully accepted by the bantam rooster and hens, and could often be seen down the backyard acting like a surrogate mother to their chicks. This was surprising as the chicks would normally be seen as a food source to a kookaburra, but Oscar had no such thoughts. Woe betide any cats or other predators that even looked at the chicks – he sent them all flying.

Oscar had also decided to appoint himself as the watchdog of our laneway beside the house. This proved to be very unfortunate for the bakery's delivery girl. He watched her enter the front gate, and then set off along the ground, beak extended, directly towards the poor girl's shins. He had never managed to fly so it was a shin-high attack. The girl screamed and I ran over and managed to get him away. The girl decided he wasn't vicious, so she stroked him and he quietened down. After that, we were obliged to install a sign on the front gate that I don't think has ever been duplicated: 'BEWARE OF THE KOOKABURRA'.

Sadly it was his efforts to be with the bantams that led to his end. He went missing one day and we searched everywhere. A week later we discovered his fate – he had become strangled in long grass and wire netting. A sad end to a truly remarkable character.

Ken Bell
Carnarvon
Western Australia

Write to me … ✉
Ken Bell
PO Box 706
Carnavon WA 6701
Australia

The escort

While at Sheffield University, my son left his room one evening and heard sounds from the stairs. He found a female student looking frightened and distressed.

She said she had been walking back to the campus alone when, as she turned a corner, she was confronted by six youths. Knowing she couldn't outrun them, she tried to walk past when, to her horror, she noticed a large Alsatian, which she assumed belonged to the youths. But as they moved towards her, jeering, the dog suddenly turned on them and sent them scattering.

As she made her way back to the campus she was aware that the dog was following her. She got to the entrance and turned. The dog stood there, head held high, then turned and left as she murmured, 'Thank you.' She was sure the dog had spared her a worse ordeal than fright.

Muriel Mack
Stoke-on-Trent, Staffordshire
England

Gyp was Eddy's protector

She was only eight weeks old when she joined us on our farm. This small ball of fluff had no idea what an important role she would play in our lives. She was a Border collie, black with white markings. We named her Gyp.

Before long, I let Gyp tag along with me to get the two milk cows out of the herd. The motherly instinct of a cow goes into action when a dog comes close to her calf. The cows had been well acquainted with our other dog, Danny, who was killed on the road by a truck. This little puppy was a stranger to the herd so I carried Gyp as we approached them. When the two milk cows were away from the herd and walking to the barn, I let Gyp run. To my surprise she began heeling them. A Border collie is born with the herding instinct and at her tender age she was showing it. In time, Gyp became a good cattle dog and saved me many steps.

Gyp didn't like strangers, and she didn't like it when I pulled her fur as I combed burrs from her coat. Other than that she was a wonderful pet to have.

When our first son Eddy arrived we wondered how Gyp would accept this gurgling little stranger. It wasn't long before our fears were put to rest. Wherever Eddy was, Gyp would be close by watching over him. As Eddy grew, so did the bond between them. He could sit on Gyp or use her to stand by grasping her coat and pulling himself up. This was the dog that wouldn't let me comb out a burr!

When Eddy was two years old, we fenced the front lawn so that he could play in the sand pile with his toys. Of course, Gyp would sit with him.

One day Gyp came to the kitchen window, looking up at me and barking excitedly. I went outside and she quickly ran to the gate. She was barking as if she was trying to tell me something was wrong.

It certainly was! Eddy had crawled over the gate by using his little wagon as a step. He was crawling under the fence towards the pasture. The cows were right there and Lady, the sassy cow, was heading towards Eddy! I was terrified. I knew I couldn't run there fast enough. As soon as I opened the gate, Gyp dashed to Eddy's rescue just in time. She grabbed Lady by her nose, thus averting a possible tragedy.

That day, Gyp proved two things: one, she was Eddy's protector when he was in danger and, two, she was smarter than me!

Ruth Jeeves
Wolseley, Saskatchewan
Canada

Help shape the future of our books

We would love to get your feedback on new ideas that we have for the SMARTER than JACK books. We're often coming up with concepts that are sometimes wacky, sometimes not. We need your help to work out what we should and should not do!

A short questionnaire may be emailed to you when we have a big decision to make. All responses will be kept confidential. Your input will help build the future of SMARTER than JACK.

To join our test group go to www.smarterthanjack.com/mainsite/concept-testers.html

Do you have a burning question?

Have the actions of an animal baffled you recently? Chances are someone else has encountered the same situation. Send us your question and we may publish it in a future edition in the SMARTER than JACK series.

Readers will be invited to offer solutions and maybe your question will be answered. You'll also receive a complimentary copy of the book that your question is published in.

For submission information please go to page 146.

9

Heroic animals are compassionate

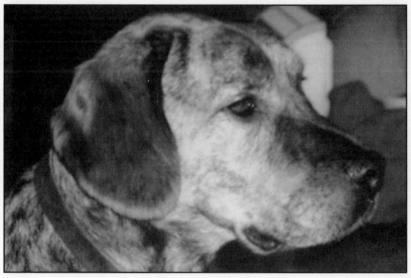

Thoughtful Timmy

All tucked in

We worked out that our 'pound puppy special' Timmy, a gorgeous auburn/brindle Staffordshire/Labrador cross, was less likely to wake us up during the night to be let outside if he was covered up with a blanket. All four sides had to be well tucked in so that he didn't get cold. When Timmy was told to go to bed, he would go and get his blanket and drag it after him so that we could tuck him in.

129

Our daughter Jessica was not feeling well and had lain down on the floor to watch television, when Timmy came into the room. He immediately left, but was back a few moments later dragging his blanket after him. He then pulled it up over Jessica and proceeded to tuck in all four corners of the blanket, one by one.

I guess Timmy thought Jessica would find being tucked in comforting too!

Wendy Gillon
West Auckland
New Zealand

A team effort

Some time ago I made a poor investment. The loss jeopardised my business and I became very depressed. One night I scarcely slept as I contemplated suicide. My plan even included having my two cats Fuzz and Twinky euthanised and cremated. Their ashes would be with me in my casket.

In the morning I got up to feed the cats and let them outside, then checked that the window they often used to enter and exit the house was open. I went back to bed.

Within five minutes Twinky came in through the window. When she noticed I was crying she sat beside me purring. A while later Fuzz came in through the window. He rubbed noses with Twinky and they had a 'catversation'. Twinky then went out the window. Fuzz nestled in beside me and purred. This went on all day. At no stage was I left alone. One cat would come in and take over the watch, and the relieved watcher would go outside for a break.

By the end of the day, I felt hungry (I had not eaten) and in a happier frame of mind. The negative thoughts had been replaced by positive strategies to develop the business and recover my financial losses. Now that has almost been achieved.

I still have Fuzz and Twinky. We're all older and wiser. Every day I give them an extra-special hug and kiss, acknowledging the occasion when they pulled me back from the brink of absolute despair.

Victoria Hunt
Hamilton
New Zealand

Magical compassion

Our beloved cocker spaniel Tammy had died that morning. After the vet's phone call I had trouble absorbing the news and longed for the feel of her soft coat. Wandering up our long drive, intending to clear any mail from our box, I stood in a daze looking along the road, so missing Tammy's company on what was one of our daily walks.

Just then, Kelly, my neighbour's springer spaniel from two doors along, came trotting towards me, not even barking. Usually, Kelly would never let me or anyone else but his owner near him. I'd always spoken to him but was always rewarded with a barrage of barking as he backed away. Today was different. He came right up to me and, as I squatted in amazement, licked my hand and then my cheek.

My heart full, and imagining this was our Tammy, I closed my eyes and Kelly let me hold his head, feel his face and ears, and enjoy his soft fur. Kelly stayed still, and when I opened my eyes he licked me

131

again and I wept and cuddled him. This was exactly what I needed, another hold of our soft, beautiful, floppy Tammy.

Kelly's owner was very surprised when I shared my experience with her. Never before or since was I able to talk to or touch Kelly without him backing away and barking.

This happened 18 years ago and I so treasure this precious memory of the generous sensitivity and understanding shown me by a neighbour's dog at the time of such grief.

Margaret Norwood
Auckland
New Zealand

Gentle Misty

It all started when my son Jason got his driver's licence at 18. He'd had his licence only two weeks when he had an accident in my car and wrecked it. As I was a divorced mother of two, the Chevy was the only car we had. My ex-husband had deserted us when my children were very young, so Jason had always considered himself to be the man in our family. This accident was a terrible blow to him. He became very depressed and did not share his feelings with anyone. He could not come to forgive himself.

My daughter Cara and I talked about what we could do to make Jason feel better; after all, accidents do happen. The decision we came to was to go the Calgary Humane Society and get him a dog. He had always wanted his own dog as Cara had a cocker spaniel named Peaches. We hoped that having a dog to talk to would help Jason.

We went to the Calgary Humane Society and picked out a sick-looking skinny dog that had the hair of a Border collie and the nose

Misty was wonderful with people

of a standard collie. She was just lying there, looking like she needed saving just as badly as Jason did. She had been brought in as a stray. The Humane Society told us that the people who had brought her in had seen someone throw her out of a car onto the road. She had just had a litter of pups and this is why she had so little hair and was so very skinny. They said she was a pure-bred tricoloured rough collie, but she sure did not look like it at the time.

We took Jason up to the Calgary Humane Society the next day and watched him go through the kennels. He picked the same dog as Cara and I had – was it fate? Misty was to be ours. The Humane Society spayed her and we brought her home. What a job that was – she was terrified to go in the car and we were terrified about picking her up as she had just had surgery.

We brought her home and laid her on the living room floor. Misty was in pretty bad shape. She was so skinny you could see her ribs, backbone and hips through her skimpy coat. Jason brought his pillow and blankets into the living room and remained by her side day and night.

We introduced Peaches to her, hoping the presence of another dog would make her feel more comfortable. Misty took to her immediately and became Peaches' adopted mother. Peaches would curl up on Misty's tummy and Misty would lick and clean Peaches' face. She would take her long slender nose and flip back one of Peaches' long ears. She would lovingly lick and clean the ear, paying attention to every nook and cranny. Then she would use her nose to flip back the other ear and clean it too. Cocker spaniels are known for ear infections but Peaches never had an ear infection in her entire life!

Misty was so terrified of the car that when we put her in it she would lose control of her bowels. All this poor dog knew was that Man had taken away her puppies, and then Man had tossed her from a car and left her to fend for herself. How could this dog ever forgive Man and learn to trust again?

It took a year of hard work, but slowly Misty gained the confidence to travel in the car. Jason took Misty with him everywhere. Once she learned that a car trip would always bring something fun, like a walk in the country, and that she would always come home with him, she learned not to fear the car so much. Slowly she quit panting and drooling, got her 'sea legs' and quit getting carsick.

With each other's love and attention, both Jason and Misty blossomed. Jason shared all his thoughts and feelings with Misty, and she in return was there for him. As she became attached to him, Misty put on weight and became playful and happy. Her coat came back and she became quite pretty and definitely looked more like a collie. By devoting his every minute to helping Misty, Jason soon forgot his own problems and blossomed into a wonderful young man, with Misty showing him the way. If she could forgive Man for all the wrongdoings in her life and trust and love again, how could Jason not forgive himself?

Peaches was enrolled in the PALS (Pet Access League Society) programme as a therapy dog. PALS critters visit people and children in nursing homes and hospitals. After we'd had Misty for a year, we decided to have her tested as well to see if she could visit with Peaches. Well, Misty passed with flying colours and now both dogs could visit together at the Glenmore Auxiliary Hospital.

On Misty's first visit she walked up to a resident's bed and put her long slender nose between the bars of the bedside railing. She laid her head on the bed and waited for the frail hand to reach her nose and pet it. How did this dog know to do that? I certainly had not trained her, and this was her first visit.

Misty became a master at visiting at the hospital. She was so patient. It's as if she knew to wait patiently for the poor crippled, shaking hands to work and reach out to her. She would sit quietly beside a wheelchair and just look at the resident until they could respond. She never scared them. She was so quiet and gentle. How she knew what each individual needed, I do not know. We would walk into the room and let Misty decide how to handle the residents.

One night Jason was out and it was just Cara, the dogs and me asleep in our town house in Calgary. Misty started running round in circles in my bedroom and barking this high-pitched urgent bark. I woke up, and just knew something was wrong by the way Misty was barking. I got up and followed her down the stairs.

As we reached the main floor I could smell the horrible smell of smoke that an electric fire gives off, coming from the basement. I ran upstairs and woke Cara and we ran out of the house with the dogs. By now the house was so filled with smoke that you could not see and the smoke detectors were ringing. We were able to shut down all the electricity and contain the fire to the basement. Misty saved me, Cara and Peaches that night – and she saved all the neighbouring town houses from burning down too!

Collies are an amazing breed. Misty has many other little stories of wonderful things she did. How did a dog that was so abused and frightened forgive us and become such a wonderful, devoted and loving member of our family? Why would this dog forgive us for what people had done to her and her puppies and bring such joy and healing to so many?

Every day I am grateful for having had Misty, and grateful to the Calgary Humane Society for letting us adopt such a wonderful dog. Maybe there is a Misty out there that could heal someone else too, if they would only give these special dogs a chance.

In remembrance of Misty.

Sandi Good
High River, Alberta
Canada

Write to me ... ✉
email Sandi
sburns65@hotmail.com

Maggie loves and protects us

Last year my son Joshua, aged six, was to come home on the school bus and be met by his grandfather. Unfortunately, his grandfather was late and Joshua found the house empty except for our 13-year-old Border collie Maggie.

Maggie was lying in her usual spot on the patio where she spent most of her time. She allowed Joshua to enter the house, but when he came out crying and upset she refused to allow him off the step. She comforted Joshua and looked after him until Grandfather arrived.

While it was only 15 minutes, I am glad that Maggie was there to protect my son and care for him in his time of need.

Carrie Knowlton
Middleton, New Brunswick
Canada

Write to me ... ✉
email Carrie
caknowlton@msn.com

Tazmo knew what I needed

Tazmo is my five-year-old Burmese cat. He is a treasured member of the family and has a weak spot for Vegemite.

As a teen, I go through a lot of different emotions on a daily basis as a part of growing up, and the pain caused by my braces often makes my life more miserable than that of my friends. But no matter how depressed or hurt I'm feeling, Tazmo is always there to give me a hug and make me feel better, and always seems to know when something disastrous has happened.

When my beloved grandma passed away early last year, everyone in the household was really sad. I felt so sad, but for some reason I could not cry. I just kept on going to school, doing homework, continuing my life, but the whole time I felt like I had lost a part of me. I would often just sit there staring at the wall, trying to comprehend what had happened and wondering when everything would go back to normal again.

When the funeral came, I thought I was OK and knew I had to give my dad moral support for the eulogy he had to give for his departed mother. However, when the time for the burial came I cried and cried and couldn't stop.

137

When I came home I was still horribly depressed. But as soon as I walked in the door, Tazmo jumped up on my shoulder – something he hadn't done since he was a kitten – and never left my side for a moment.

He was my guardian angel who helped my through this sad time, and I will always love him for the never-ending comfort he gave me in my time of need.

Simone Corletto
Adelaide
South Australia

Write to me … ✉

email Simone
tiger_cub684@hotmail.com

My Boo knew just what to do

Boo was a big Airedale terrier, a gentle giant of about 90 pounds. I lived in an urban area and right next door to me lived a little boy, Timmy (not his real name), and his grandpa. Timmy was an overweight boy, and about seven years old at the time of this story.

One day Timmy was playing in my yard with Boo. His grandpa came out of his house and – it was awful – he yelled at Timmy, 'Get out of that yard before that dog bites you.'

Timmy said, 'Grandpa, Boo would never bite me, he loves me.'

Grandpa, believe it or not, said, 'Dogs hate fat kids and you are fat.'

I said to my neighbour, 'I don't think you understand what you are saying to your grandson.'

He said, 'Yes, the kid is fat and the dog is going to bite him.'

Timmy went and lay down on our lawn chair and closed his eyes. I was trying to think what to say to comfort this poor kid, when

Boo went and laid his big head on Timmy's chest. Timmy opened his eyes and said, 'I knew you loved me, Boo!' and everything was all right for them.

Boo seemed to know just what to do. What a dog!

Cherie Gabriel
Northport, Michigan
United States of America

Write to me ... ✉
email Cherie
cg72148@bignet.net

Dusters seemed to understand

I have a beautiful three-year-old tan Staffy called Dusters, whom I bought with my now former partner. My partner was in the navy at the time and was due to travel to Iraq for six months.

Dusters was about six or seven months old when my partner made his trip. I had seen him off at the wharf in Sydney, which was a very emotional affair. Later that evening I was home watching the news and they featured a story about my partner's ship leaving for Iraq, which upset me all over again.

As I sat crying, Dusters – who had previously been asleep at the end of the bed – got up, came over and sat in my lap and leaned into me as if to comfort me.

Of course this made me cry harder, but I felt an immense amount of gratitude for his intuition. He understood my pain and wanted to make me feel better.

Shannon Curtis
Terrigal, New South Wales
Australia

Dusters used his intuition

Mishka shows her sensitive side

I always thought that Mishka, a black part-Siamese cat named after the Russian Olympics bear symbol, was arrogant, aloof and bossy. Then one day she showed her sensitive side.

In December 1991 I had an accident with our new safety-wire door. It closed too quickly on my slipper heel, throwing me sideways on the floor. My hip was fractured in the fall. When I came home from hospital I had a plate and screws in my hip and had to use crutches for three months.

For a few days our other two cats – Chance, an attractive white, black and grey tabby, and her sister Rascal, a grey and black tabby – kept well away from me after a few tentative sniffs.

I had to do gentle leg exercises on the bed four times a day. The first time I did this I must have given a little groan because, the next thing I knew, a warm black body had sprung onto the pillow beside me. Mishka leaned over and I felt her whiskers gently brush my face as she peered into my eyes and then gently licked my chin. I am sure she was saying in cat language, *I am here with you and will watch over you.*

Isabel Mealand
East Malvern, Victoria
Australia

Write to me ... ✉
Mrs Isabel Mealand
16 Grant Street
East Malvern VIC 3145
Australia

Fluffy earned his keep ... and more

My husband, who was retired, always said he didn't really like cats and would never have one. The little kitten next door took no notice of that silly business. He would come in every day and follow my husband everywhere he went. He became Dick's cat – or was it the other way round?

My husband died suddenly from a heart attack when Fluffy was nine months old. Fluffy stayed on and was much loved, though he was never really affectionate. He would tolerate being picked up for a cuddle but made his getaway as soon as possible. He wasn't big but he was very smart and a terrific mouser and rat catcher. He definitely earned his keep.

When I came home after an operation that left me very sick, he followed me everywhere and would sit close and put his head in my

141

lap. He had never done this before and I'm sure he knew how sick I was. I recovered, and Fluffy lived until he was over 20. I have lovely memories of him.

Pearl Hunter
Burwood, Victoria
Australia

Write to me ... ✉
Pearl Hunter
6 Harrison Avenue
Burwood VIC 3125
Australia

Like what you're reading? Tell us your favourite story

We hope you've enjoyed reading about heroic animals. We'd love to know which story is your favourite. This will help us choose the stories for future 'best of' editions of SMARTER than JACK.

Please write the book, page number and story title on the back of an envelope or postcard. You will go into the draw to win a one-year subscription to the SMARTER than JACK series. There will be a draw every time a new book is released and the winner will be announced in our 'Celebrate Animals' newsletter.

For submission information please go to page 146.

The SMARTER than JACK story

We hope you've enjoyed this book. The SMARTER than JACK books are exciting and entertaining to create and so far we've raised over NZ$320,000 to help animals. We are thrilled!

Here's my story about how the SMARTER than JACK series came about.

Until late 1999 my life was a seemingly endless search for the elusive 'fulfilment'. I had this feeling that I was put on this earth to make a difference, but I had no idea how. Coupled with this, I had low self-confidence – not a good combination! This all left me feeling rather frustrated, lonely and unhappy with life. I'd always had a creative streak and loved animals. In my early years I spent many hours designing things such as horse saddles, covers and cat and dog beds. I even did a stint as a professional pet photographer.

Then I remembered something I was once told: do something for the right reasons and good things will come. So that's what I did. I set about starting Avocado Press and creating the first New Zealand edition in the SMARTER than JACK series. It was released in 2002 and all the profit went to the Royal New Zealand SPCA.

Good things did come. People were thrilled to be a part of the book and many were first-time writers. Readers were enthralled and many were delighted to receive the book as a gift from friends and family. The Royal New Zealand SPCA was over $43,000 better off and I received many encouraging letters and emails from readers and contributors. What could be better than that?

How could I stop there! It was as if I had created a living thing with the SMARTER than JACK series; it seemed to have a life all of its own. I now had the responsibility of evolving it. It had to continue to benefit animals and people by providing entertainment, warmth and something that people could feel part of. What an awesome responsibility and opportunity, albeit a bit of a scary one!

It is my vision to make SMARTER than JACK synonymous with smart animals, and a household name all over the world. The concept is already becoming well known as a unique and effective way for animal welfare charities to raise money, to encourage additional donors and to instil a greater respect for animals. The series is now in Australia, New Zealand, the United States of America, Canada and the United Kingdom.

Avocado Press, as you may have guessed, is a little different. We are about more than just creating books; we're about sharing information and experiences, and developing things in innovative ways. Ideas are most welcome too.

We feel it's possible to run a successful business that is both profitable and that contributes to animal welfare in a significant way. We want people to enjoy and talk about our books; that way, ideas are shared and the better it becomes for everyone.

Thank you for reading my story.

Jenny Campbell
Creator of SMARTER than JACK

Submit a story for our books

We are always creating more exciting books in the SMARTER than JACK series. Your true stories are continually being sought.

You can have a look at our website www.smarterthanjack.com. Here you can read stories, find information on how to submit stories, and read entertaining and interesting animal news. You can also sign up to receive the Story of the Week by email. We'd love to hear your ideas, too, on how to make the next books even better.

Guidelines for stories

- The story must be true and about a smart animal or animals.
- The story should be about 100 to 1000 words in length. We may edit it and you will be sent a copy to approve prior to publication.
- The story must be written from your point of view, not the animal's.
- Photographs and illustrations are welcome if they enhance the story, and if used will most likely appear in black and white.
- Submissions can be sent by post to SMARTER than JACK (see addresses on the following page) or via the website at www.smarterthanjack.com.
- Include your name, postal and email address, and phone number, and indicate if you do not wish your name to be included with your story.
- Handwritten submissions are perfectly acceptable, but if you can type them, so much the better.
- Posted submissions will not be returned unless a stamped self-addressed envelope is provided.
- The writers of stories selected for publication will be notified prior to publication.
- Stories are welcome from everybody, and given the charitable nature of our projects there will be no prize money awarded, just recognition for successful submissions.

- Particpating animal welfare charities and Avocado Press have the right to publish extracts from the stories received without restriction of location or publication, provided the publication of those extracts helps promote the SMARTER than JACK series.

Where to send your submissions

Online

- Use the submission form at www.smarterthanjack.com or email it to submissions@smarterthanjack.com

By post

- **In Australia**
  PO Box 170, Ferntree Gully, VIC 3156, Australia
- **In Canada and the United States of America**
  PO Box 819, Tottenham, ON, L0G 1W0, Canada
- **In New Zealand and rest of world**
  PO Box 27003, Wellington, New Zealand

Don't forget to include your contact details. Note that we may use the information you provide to send you further information about the SMARTER than JACK series. If you do not wish for us to do this, please let us know.

Receive a SMARTER than JACK gift pack

Did you know that around half our customers buy the SMARTER than JACK books as gifts? We appreciate this and would like to thank and reward those who do so. If you buy eight books in the SMARTER than JACK series we will send you a free gift pack.

All you need to do is buy your eight books and either attach the receipt for each book or, if you ordered by mail, just write the date that you placed the order in one of the spaces on the next page. Then complete your details on the form, cut out the page and post it to us. We will then send you your SMARTER than JACK gift pack. Feel free to photocopy this form – that will save cutting a page out of the book.

Do you have a dog or a cat? You can choose from either a cat or dog gift pack. Just indicate your preference.

Note that the contents of the SMARTER than JACK gift pack will vary from country to country, but may include:
- The SMARTER than JACK mini Collector Series
- SMARTER than JACK postcards
- Soft animal toy
- Books in the SMARTER than JACK series

Show your purchases here:

Book 1	Book 2	Book 3	Book 4
Receipt attached ☐ *or* Date ordered _____	Receipt attached ☐ *or* Date ordered _____	Receipt attached ☐ *or* Date ordered _____	Receipt attached ☐ *or* Date ordered _____
Book 5	Book 6	Book 7	Book 8
Receipt attached ☐ *or* Date ordered _____	Receipt attached ☐ *or* Date ordered _____	Receipt attached ☐ *or* Date ordered _____	Receipt attached ☐ *or* Date ordered _____

Complete your details:

Your name: _____
Street address: _____
City/town: _____
State: _____
Postcode: _____
Country: _____
Phone: _____
Email: _____
Would you like a cat or dog gift pack?   CAT/DOG

Post the completed page to us:

- **In Australia**
  PO Box 170, Ferntree Gully, VIC 3156, Australia
- **In Canada and the United States of America**
  PO Box 819, Tottenham, ON, L0G 1W0, Canada
- **In New Zealand and rest of world**
  PO Box 27003, Wellington, New Zealand
Please allow four weeks for delivery.

Which animal charities do we help?

At SMARTER than JACK we work with many charities around the world. Below is a list of some of the charities that benefit from the sale of our books. For a more complete list please visit www.smarterthanjack.com. If would like your charity to benefit from SMARTER than JACK please contact Angela Robinson by email: angela@smarterthanjack.com.

New Zealand

Royal New Zealand SPCA and their branches and member societies: www.rspca.org.nz

Australia

RSPCA Australia and their eight state and territory member societies: www.rspca.org.au

United Kingdom

- Cats Protection: www.cats.org.uk
- Dogs for the Disabled: www.dogsforthedisabled.org
- Dogs Trust: www.dogstrust.org.uk

Canada

The Canadian Federation of Humane Societies and their participating member societies: www.cfhs.ca

United States of America

PETA (People for the Ethical Treatment of Animals) www.peta.org and around 25 Humane Societies, Welfare Leagues and SPCAs from all over the United States of America.

Get more wonderful stories

Now you can receive a fantastic new-release SMARTER than JACK book every three months. That's a new book every March, June, September and December. The books are delivered to your door. It's easy!

Every time you get a book you will also receive a copy of *Celebrate Animals*, our members-only newsletter. Postage is included in the subscription price if the delivery address is in Canada, the United Kingdom, Australia or New Zealand.

You can also purchase existing titles in the SMARTER than JACK series. To purchase a book go to your local bookstore or visit our website **www.smarterthanjack.com** and select the participating charity that you would like to benefit from your purchase.

How your purchase will help animals

The amount our partner animal welfare charities receive varies according to how the books are sold and the country in which they are sold. Contact your local participating animal welfare charity for more information.

Story postcard

Send this story postcard to a fellow animal lover and spread the smart animal message.

Fold along the perforated line and carefully tear out your story postcard.

To order more story postcards go to www.smarterthanjack.com.

A smart animal story for you ...

A short time ago I purchased a 'Busy Box' toy to keep my cats occupied and amused. It worked and they all seemed to enjoy it.

One day I was watching them play and noticed that all the toys had been batted out of the box. Zane (an eight-month-old kitten) proceeded to go around the room collecting the toys and carrying them back to put them in the holes of the Busy Box. Then they all continued with their game.

Sharon Irwin
USA

SMARTER
THAN
JACK®

The books series that helps animals & connects animal lovers worldwide

www.smarterthanjack.com

rachaelhale®

The world's most lovable animals